Stuff I've Never Told Anyone

Finding Power in the Shadow of Shame

An Anthology of Anonymous Stories,

Poems, and Letters

Amy R Brooks

Stuff I've Never

Told Anyone

© *2017*

VoicePenPurpose™ Publishing

Cover Design by Abe Kane

Dedication

To all the women who are ready

to stand up to Shame

and connect with their Power.

Table of Contents

Preface

Women come together for many reasons. We love to have fun, laugh, and encourage one another. We feel needed when friends are looking for reassurance or some sassy advice.

Women understand that sadness and pain are a part of our experience, but we don't often share the stories of shame.

Pain and shame can show up differently.

Shame carries an additional weight that is too heavy to bring to a Girls' Night Out. Shame isn't appropriate for a quick coffee date. Shame is often too buried and partially forgotten. It hides away under the reality we embrace on a daily basis. Shame is in our closet, buried under the many boxes of memories that have formed who we are, but it's rarely removed or put on display for others to see.

Then what becomes of shame?

Does it grow or shrink over time?

Could it get old and die or does it live an eternal life within our subconscious?

For the many women featured in this book, the answers vary. They have gone into the closet and searched through the piles of dusty, stale memories that have spanned their lifetime. By contributing to this book they have begun a quest to find the origin of the story surrounding their general feelings of shame. In the midst of daily life and normalcy, they decided that *now* was the time to clean up the stacks of ideas and experiences that made them feel inferior; separate.

Each contributor chose not to question how the "right time" suddenly arrived in her life, instead she opened the door and stepped to the side as the feelings of shame waited for her on the other side of the doorway. No one wanted to undermine the wisdom of the moment, but each woman was nervously aware that she was about to invite an almost palpable Shame into her awareness. This was an opportunity to finally understand the role of Shame in her life and the lessons that came from that understanding were too important to be ignored. She braced herself and looked at Shame; really allowed herself to see all angles of its form.

She took in its presence and its influence. She sized it up and decided that she was ready to sit down with this Shame and talk to it about its birth and subsequent impact.

On some level, each writer acknowledged that Shame was real in her life. It was before her; whole, complete, alive. For its part, the Shame felt, ironically, unashamed. In fact, it felt welcome and important. It was confident that it was necessary.

Its certainty became its demise. The Shame that always held power suddenly felt unstable. Even in those opening moments of examination, something started shifting. Nothing about Shame could change, so it looked outside of itself...to her. Each writer looked at Shame head-on. Her head slightly cocked to the left and her eyes narrowed. What was this Shame? Had she ever really understood why it was here? Why had she invited it; why had she let it live with her?

Shame squirmed under examination. It didn't know its purpose under these new circumstances. She had never looked at it with so much energy. Shame never wants scrutiny or analysis. Shame appreciated averted gazes and whispered asides. But she *didn't* look away and she didn't whisper.

"Why are you here?" she asked with an even tone.

Shame looked around. Who was she talking to?

"I know you heard me. Why are you here, Shame?"

"Uh…" Shame had never been asked this.

"What is your purpose? How are you helping me? I need to know," she pressed with eyes narrowing.

"You invited me in, so I came," it finally replied with a shrug.

"I invited you?"

"Yes."

"But why would I invite you?"

"You said I was necessary."

"Are you?"

"Sure."

"Why?"

"Because you said so. You know what you need. If you say I'm necessary, then I must be important. I did what you wanted me to do," Shame retorted.

"But why would I want shame in my life?" she asked again. Her expression was both curious and confused, as if she wanted to know the answer to a question she didn't understand.

"I guess I help people make sense of a situation. I give them a way to categorize things no one talks about."

"Things we don't talk about?" she repeated.

"You know.

"No, I'm not sure if I do."

"The stuff no one ever talks about: being hurt, making mistakes that hurt others, witnessing others hurt people. I show up when you don't know what you did wrong, but you know you feel separate from others. You know, those times when you have broken the contract."

"Contract? I never signed a contract."

"But you did. A long time ago you were clean and whole and wise. In that moment you promised yourself that you would never forget your connection to all things. You made a contract, a pact, a covenant; whatever you want to call it. Your soul said you would stay connected and in the moment that connection was severed you invited me in. I don't always know why I show up, I'm just called forth. I go where I'm called. I fill in the gaps when the connection is broken."

"You fill in the gaps?" she was thinking now.

"Yes."

"So that's the only option, to invite in shame."

"Well there is some comfort in my shadow."

"The shadow of shame," she pieced together for herself.

"Yes."

"But that's not the only option. I know it. What aren't you telling me?"

"Well, you always can choose another path," Shame admitted.

"I can? We can? Everyone?"

"Yes, of course. But I can assure you that it is far scarier than I am."

She looked at Shame, now sitting heavily before her. The weight of it overwhelmed her and she wished it was gone. She couldn't imagine anything worse than what was before her now. The darkness Shame brought with its presence was oppressive. Nothing could be worse. Shame was lying to her. She was sure of it.

"You're lying," she announced flatly.

"No, I'm not. Most people *choose* me. They know they can count on me. It's easier this way."

"Some other path," she repeated, ignoring his self-defense. "You said we have some other option. So that means I can *choose* something other than shame?"

"Yes," Shame confirmed.

"Then tell me. Tell me what's worse than you that hardly anyone chooses."

"Reconnection."

"Reconnection?" she questioned.

"Yes, you can choose to reconnect; to honor your human contract. You can choose to reconnect to life and joy and hope. You can trust your wisdom and know that you are clean and whole."

"But what if that's no longer true for me? What if things have happened that make that not true? What if I'm no longer clean and whole because of things that have happened? What if I can no longer trust my wisdom?"

"It's never *not* true, you just separate from that knowing. You choose to forget that you can always connect to love. When that happens, I come to fill in the gap. I'm there in the spaces where reconnection is not welcome."

"And if I choose to reconnect? What happens then?"

Shame looked up, meeting her eyes, "Oh, if you choose love, then you will become more powerful than you ever thought possible."

Shame paused.

"...and there will be no room for me."

"Nothing haunts us like the things we don't say."

Mitch Albom

Checkmate

Maribel

I used to drink quite a bit when I was in college. I was a social drinker, but I went out every day, so I drank every day. I thought I was becoming an alcoholic, which scared me, so I stopped drinking so much.

In 2006, six months after graduating from college, I landed a corporate job. This new role had me training away from home for nine weeks.

The last day of training would be easy. Half day recap, lunch, goodbyes, whatever.

I was tired of living out of a hotel room, I missed home, I was ready to go back home as soon as they let us out. I was anxious to hit the road.
The night before I was scheduled to leave, I went out with a friend. We planned an early night, the next morning I had work and a 9 hour drive. We celebrated that we had made it, that we had finally become adults.

At the bar, we had two Coronas each.

I was always aware of my surroundings, never took my eyes off of my drink, never set it down, and I'd watch the bartender open or pour my drink. We all know the drill.

So we danced, we laughed, we celebrated our success as Mexican-American first-generation college graduates with professional jobs. We were going to be unstoppable.

A couple of very attractive men came over. They were very well dressed and the way they carried themselves inspired our trust. They offered to buy us drinks and we refused. We were already on our second beer and almost ready to take off, so they bought us bottled water. I kept my thumb on the opening after losing the cap. You can never be too safe.

I don't remember what happened next. There is a gap between a blurry walk outside the bar and the next morning.

I woke up shivering, confused, with an ever-widening hole in my memory. I was lying on a shiny white ceramic tile floor. It took me a while to realize it was a bathroom. I got up and stumbled, I had to hold the wall with both hands in order to not fall. My pants were down around my ankles. My hair was messy, my shirt was halfway unbuttoned, my mind and body were numb. I washed my hands and saw myself in the mirror. My makeup was smeared and I noticed dried up mascara down my cheeks showing traces of my tears.

I didn't understand.

I left the bathroom and didn't recognize the house, nor could I remember who I was with. Nothing made sense, but I was so out of it that I wasn't even scared, just confused.

I opened the door to a bedroom and there was my friend. Fully clothed with her coat on, asleep in a bed. An unknown man was sleeping next to her in nothing but his boxers. He was spooning her. I shook her awake and although she seemed confused, she knew we had to leave.

Her keys were on the nightstand next to her purse.

She walked out first, looking like a zombie. We went straight for the front door. I tried to pay attention to my surroundings to make sense of the situation we were in when I noticed several condoms on the floor that I hadn't seen when I left the bathroom. There were empty bottles of beer on the living room floor and a half empty bottle of tequila on the table.

I also noticed a glass chess set. It reminded me, in a flash, of my childhood. I used to be a competitive chess player. From the age of 8-years old, I knew how to play the game to win. I was one of only three students in my class who was allowed compete against our teacher. It was through challenge and adversity that I learned to be strategic. To this day I find myself looking at every situation and calculating my next five moves.

This instinct served me well as I continued assess our situation. I knew we had to leave immediately, so I didn't hesitate to follow my friend out the door.

We found her truck in the parking garage by pressing the panic button on the alarm remote key and I drove us out. She sat in the truck without moving, without saying anything; she didn't know where she was. Eventually I recognized a major street and figured out how to get back. I dropped my friend off at her house. Not a single word was said, and then I drove to my hotel. I went up to my room and got in bed.

I thought I was dreaming. I heard a faraway noise that wouldn't go away. I woke up to my phone ringing. I sat up on the bed and saw I had ten missed calls from a coworker. The phone rang again and I answered. He asked what happened but I didn't know what he meant. We were supposed to carpool to work that morning after having breakfast together, but I never showed up at the time we had agreed on. He told our supervisor that I had woken up very ill and that I would show up a couple of hours late.

I told him I would get ready and go, but went back to sleep after hanging up. An hour later, my phone rang again.

"What the hell is going on, Rubio? What happened to you? Are you drunk?"

"No, of course I'm not drunk! I had two beers last night and that was around 8."

"Then what the fuck? I lied for you at work. We're in groups and they're looking for you. If you don't come in they're gonna go to your room to make sure you're okay. Get your ass here now!"

"Okay fine, I'm on my way."

I brushed my hair and teeth, washed my face, and went to work. I knew I was walking but couldn't feel my feet moving. I knew I was on my way to work, yet nothing was clicking in my mind. Everything felt like a dream, like an alternate reality where you are not who you really are and you can almost see yourself doing everything in slow motion.

I went inside the conference room and sat next to my coworker. The supervisor asked if I was fine and if I needed anything. I must've looked pathetic because everyone looked at me with pity in their eyes. I could tell that I still wasn't all there.

I sat in silence staring at my knockoff Gucci bag emblem. The Gs on the bag appeared to be moving slowly into a circle that would eventually turn into a vortex, a vortex that consumed all of the adjacent Gs. I closed my eyes and I could see Gs moving in all directions, dancing. My friend asked me to go to the bathroom, drink some water or coffee, and snap out of it.

As I sat on the toilet seat, I had an overwhelming desire to cry, to scream, to pull my hair out but I did not know why, and the physical reactions would not come. I wiped and saw blood on the toilet paper and with that almost seemingly insignificant cue, I felt stabbing pain in my anus. It was as if that entire time I had been falling from a building, no emotion, no feeling, no concept of time or reality and seeing the blood was like hitting the floor. My entire body ached. I had a hard time getting up because my legs were shaking,I was shivering, and in an instant I was bawling and couldn't breathe. I went to the mirror and I looked like shit. My hair was somewhat brushed, I was wearing the same clothes from the previous night, my shirt was wrinkled, and my face had day-old makeup that had lasted through the night. I washed my hands and my face and tried to fix my hair and clothes as best I could.

Walking back to the conference room was difficult. I sat next to my friend and he immediately confirmed his suspicions that something was definitely wrong.

"Are you on drugs? Goddamn it, Rubio, did you take any drugs?" he whispered and then sighed. "Or did someone give you something?"

Tears started rolling down my face. He gave me a napkin he had serving as a cookie holder and rubbed my back gently and slowly. I could see his jaw clenching. In the two months we had spent together we'd become very close. He tried to touch my leg to comfort me and I flinched instinctively. He already knew what had happened, even before I did.

I knew I was in pain. I felt lost and nothing made sense. But the second I felt his hand on my leg I was hit with flashbacks.

I was back in that apartment. I saw myself sitting on a couch with two young men, one on each side. We were playing chess and they were drinking tequila. I was good at chess and somehow they beat me. I heard one say, "Checkmate" and then his hands were on me.

Black out.

I saw myself on the bathroom floor, I couldn't move my body, I couldn't talk, only feel. It hurts. I try to push him away but I'm not strong enough. My words are slurred "No... don't... stop..... NO!" My knees are hurting, my bad knee, the right one, is really throbbing. He is pushing himself inside me violently. All I can do at this time is hold on to the tub as best I can so he doesn't smash my face on it with each thrust. It hurts so much, but resisting hurts way more. I let myself go.

Black out.

Our supervisors at work let us out early because some people had to catch a flight. I stay for two more nights. My friend takes me to his room and makes me sleep in his bed while he sleeps on the couch. He doesn't want to leave me alone, but also doesn't want to get too close.

I replay the scenes over and over. I should not have gone. I shouldn't have had *anything* to drink. I must've removed my thumb from the bottle at *some* point. Did I drink that tequila willingly? We were at *their* place, what does that mean? Did I lead them on? But I'm a fucking lesbian, I don't even like men! Goddamn it, why did I have to go out? Why did this happen to me? I am so stupid! I am such a fucking idiot! This is all my fault, oh god, this is all my fault. I don't even know who these people are, where they live, their names, what they were driving, how tall they were, NOTHING!

I don't go to the cops.

I don't go to the hospital.

I drive home and cry the entire way back. It takes me eleven hours.

It takes me two weeks to recover, like a bad hangover, from whatever they gave me.

It takes me months to be able to be intimate with my girlfriend, with the woman that loves me so tenderly. She is so nurturing, so caring. The first thing she said while embracing me tightly and clenching her jaw was, "It *wasn't* your fault." I didn't believe her then.

It took me ten years before I could look at men without a defensive strategy in mind. I was always on guard. It also took me ten years to believe that none of it was my fault. It took that decade before I could have sexual encounters without being triggered. Knowing that it wasn't my fault was one of the first steps to healing, and that healing has empowered me to return 100% to myself.

Even after all those years, there was a series of moves that society didn't see coming. I expected to be broken and weak, but the opposite happened. It wasn't checkmate. Instead, I got my queen from out of nowhere and blocked their threat to the king and obliterated their entire game. I won my power back.

I might have been another statistic, but I will not be shamed.

I might have been a victim, but I will not be victimized.

I will use my experience for awareness.

It was not my fault.

It was *NOT* your fault.

I will call out rape jokers, victim blamers, and slut-shamers.

I am a champion.

I own the board.

I choose which pieces of my life I want to save and which ones I want to advance.

I have all the power to make the next move.

Burdens Such as Mine

Ava

There are two verses in the Bible, Psalm 56:3-4, that say, "When I am afraid, I put my trust in you. In God, whose word I praise, in God I trust; I shall not be afraid. What can flesh do to me?"

I have a lot of fears, some of which have been disabling at some point in my life, but I have adapted to a new philosophy: when there is a Goliath in front of me, there is a David inside of me. Nothing, however, has scared me more in my life than the thought of someone, anyone, learning who I really am. Nothing is more terrifying than someone knowing the deepest secrets of my soul and seeing the person behind the smile, for therein lies a woman who has buried her secrets and bares her burdens like prison shackles, all with hope for true freedom.

I have been strong all my life, having had to learn how to be strong to do what I always felt called to do, and that is to change the world through empowerment and compassion. The need to remain light, joyous, and courageous, has molded me into a person with many strengths and many weaknesses. I have also experienced a lot of changes and trauma in my life, with those experiences giving me my ability to keep moving along as if nothing will stop me, because it will not.

I do not remember how old I was when the defining incident happened; I did not even remember anything had happened until recently. As a child, I was taught where my private parts are, to never let anyone touch me there. I was taught that I should turn to family members when something is not okay. What happens, though, when someone repeatedly hurts you, but you do not want to cause any more trouble in your household? There are already enough arguments, fights, and alcohol-fueled daggers thrown. These incidents feel like they're entirely your fault, because you are the brat who cannot contain your anger. You are the brat who is constantly getting into trouble at school and being sent to institutes to be evaluated. So you keep the new problems to yourself; you do not need to burden anyone else with even more of your problems.

He was six years older than me and he was crossing that threshold into his teenage years, while

I was still a young girl with no knowledge or experience about exploring sexuality. We were close; almost like family. Sometimes when we were alone, he would show me pornographic pictures and films, but that turned into taking his privates out and forcing me to watch what happens when he gets "excited." Sometimes he touched me and did things in both my private area, and my developing chest. I did not know it was wrong, but I did know it did not feel right to me. It made me feel horrible and dirty, but I could not tell anyone. To this day, I still have not told another person.

To this day, I get scared when lovers touch me. I do not even like being caressed by a man. I feel like I am unlovable because I cannot enjoy being with another person. It is too complicated to love someone with secrets so deep that they cannot tell you what exactly prevents them from engaging in activities that should be pleasurable and fun.

I have been through a lot in my life, yet no hands, no words, and no actions have damaged my health more than this. Nothing has shaped me more than the sexual abuse I experienced. I cannot even share this story with people in my life, because I cannot let go of the secret.

The shame has held me back more than any other obstacle, and I do not know where to go from here. What I do know, though, is that by sharing my story now, something may shift. Maybe someone else in the world can free themselves from burdens such as mine. Even if I am not totally free from my shame, I am healing myself a little bit more each day. That healing is, in itself, a very powerful next step for me.

"I told her once I wasn't good at anything. She told me survival is a talent."

Susanna Kaysen

Love is a
Multifaceted Word

Amelia

How do I tell you how much you are loved? I planned you from the very beginning. I took ovulation tests to verify when would be the best time to conceive you. I still remember how I wanted two kids more than anything; two kids, who could grow up together, learn together, test each other and be there for each other.

It worked.

Four weeks after trying to conceive you, I had confirmation that you were real. You were on your way to complete us as a family. You were the missing piece that would tie us altogether for a life time of happily ever after. Two days later, I almost lost you. The feeling of pride vanished. The feeling of ultimate love, extinguished. The feeling that my happily ever after had been ripped from my heart. I was alone and scared and so very sad. How could it be FAIR that the love I felt for you, now had no basis, because you might be gone? After several days and several tests, still mentally and physically alone, I was told that you were still there with me. The feeling of relief was overwhelming.

I did everything by the book and held myself to a standard of extreme well-being, so that you too could be as perfect as I imagined you to be. Perfection; however, was my demise. I wasn't perfect and my marriage was far from perfect. After you decided to stay, I came to a life-altering realization that although you would be perfect, I was not, and this marriage was not, and life was far from it.

Another mental shift, and I needed out. I needed to get as far away as I could from my reality, from the life that had consumed me, but did not represent me. I decided to take a mental vacation and imagined that you didn't exist. I even reminded myself that you didn't have to exist, because if I wanted to, I could end your existence. I could make sure that you would never materialize and I wouldn't have to be stuck in this cycle. I would have an escape route.

From that moment on, I was no longer kind to my mind, my body, or my soul – I was too broken to face what I had become and what I was bringing you into. Running away did not clear my mind, but opened it to the truth of what I had become and what I needed to be. It was difficult to face. I suddenly realized I didn't want to go home to a life I no longer wanted.

I felt forced to choose. I had a choice to ignore my truth and sink deeper into my abyss, or face my truth and hope for both of us that there would be light at the end of the tunnel.

As I look at your sweet face, your amazingly innocent eyes, feel your breath on my shoulder, and get to know this little man that you have become, again I am overwhelmed. You saved me. You kept me going when I entered the darkness. It's hard to imagine now that I once thought about putting out your light. Your love for me is endless, yet I considered cutting off that love before it had the chance to grow.

The overwhelming feeling I have now is guilt. There is no reason, no explanation, that I could use to justify ending your life before it began. Ironically, your life saved my life. I go through each day thankful for the love we have and I promise to be a better person. I want to be more understanding and more patient. I vow to never stop learning. I want to better myself, so that you have a role model to look up to and be proud of. Although the nightmares haven't stopped, you are the calm in this storm and keep me focused. I know now that together we will find that light at the end of this long tunnel.

Still Healing

Cecilia

April 9, 2003

Dear Diary,

Well, they forgot another birthday. I don't know why I'm surprised. I don't know why I get my hopes up, why can't they acknowledge me? Why do I have to remind them it's my birthday? Why does it take someone else wishing their oldest child and only daughter happy birthday for them to remember? It's just my brother and me, it's not like they have to remember the birthdays of ten kids. However, I could bet you a million dollars that mom at church with 14 kids knows every birthday and makes them a cake or something so they each feel special. For crying out loud, it's my 13th birthday! I'm a teenager! Isn't this one of those milestone birthdays? Oh, and get this, not only do my lovely parents forget it's my birthday, but it's also not about me. My father, aka Jerk, always gets to pick where we go to dinner. Why can't I choose where I want to go for my birthday dinner? I'm not asking to go to Outback or some other fancy place.

Just once I'd like to choose. But, as always and as you well know diary, everything in life is always about him.

Thanks for being my only friend right now. My friends wouldn't understand. I'm sure their parents remember their birthdays! Shoot, a lot of them have birthday parties, cool birthday parties! I'm lucky if I'm told happy birthday ON my birthday, let alone have a few friends over to celebrate. We're not poor and I know well enough we are certainly not rich either! I'm just asking for friends to come over and eat cake with me. Is that a crime?

Thanks for listening, well I guess you don't have ears...I can't say thanks for reading because you don't have eyes...I guess thanks for being here, diary. Now's it's time to pray and talk to God.

April 12, 2003

Dear Diary,

I got my so-called birthday present from my father, aka Jerk. Except, I certainly prefer gifts that are wrapped. It's fun and exciting to not know what is inside the wrapping paper. This present was not wrapped. This present I wish I could give back. I didn't ask for it. It wasn't on my wish list, although my parents hardly pay attention to my wish list anyways. Why do they even bother asking me what I want for my birthday or Christmas if they are just going to get me whatever they want?

This gift I don't think anyone would ask for. He did something you are supposed to wait for until you get married or if you choose to sin and do it with your boyfriend or girlfriend before you get married. I heard him open my bedroom door. I had just drifted off to sleep and I was pretending to be sleeping once I heard him come in. I figured he was going to see if I was awake and yell at me for not taking out the trash like last week. Nope, that wasn't it. He laid down in my bed. I thought this was a little strange, I mean I can't remember the last time he laid down with me. Maybe when I was 7 and puking my guts out from the flu. I thought maybe he felt sorry for forgetting my milestone birthday.

Then he whispered in my ear, "if you make any noise and wake your brother or mother I'll make sure you never see the light of day".

Oh Diary...I was so scared. I know he owns a gun and he knows how to use it. I don't think he brought anything into my room with him, but I was pretending to sleep so I couldn't have been sure. I just said "okay" and laid there. I knew I had to fight back the tears because he would have smacked me in the head if I started to cry like he did two weeks ago when I started to cry because he was screaming and yelling at mom for coming home a little late after work.

We did it. You know, had sex. At least I think it was sex. I remember those classes at church where we talk about the stories from the Bible. There were sessions once we got to a certain age where we talked about our bodies changing and going through puberty, the different male and female parts and sex. He put his you-know-what inside my you-know-what. It hurt. I didn't like it. I wanted him to stop, he kept it in there and started kissing me. He never kisses me. And I'm not just talking about a kiss on the cheek or forehead like he does in front of my grandparents. He put his tongue in my mouth. I didn't know what to do. I just kept my mouth open. When he stopped after what seemed like hours he started to touch my chest. I already don't like my chest and wear sports bras all the time because most of my friends still have a flat chest. Why do I have these boob things and my friends don't? It's not fair. He was flicking them and kissing them. I just laid there and kept hoping God would stop him. I don't know how long it was but at some point he stopped everything and before he left he whispered, "I dare you to tell someone. They would never believe you, you little lying bitch. Besides, this won't be the last time. Sweet dreams and happy birthday." He left my room and I tried to listen for my parents' bedroom door to shut. I started to cry as softly as possible into my pillow. I didn't want him to hear me.

Diary, what do I do? I know what I'm NOT going to do. I can't tell anyone. I was afraid to write to you, too. He never comes in my room, so I thought. What does he mean by "this won't be the last time"? Do I have to go through that again? He is married to mom. I don't understand. I thought people had sex to make babies. I want babies, but not at 13. Can I have babies at 13? I need answers. When I'm finished writing I'm going to pray like I always do but I know God can't talk to me just like you. Just another day in the life of me I guess.

10 years later

April 2, 2013

Dear Diary,

I can't believe after all these years I'm still writing to you. I started when I was 9 with a few doodles and notes here and there. I wrote a lot between 12 and 15 years old. I know I let it go to the wayside for a little while, but now at almost 23 I'm trying to write at least two times a week. I think it will be helpful. When my therapist told me to try journaling, I remembered how much I liked writing as an adolescent so I figured why not as an adult. I'm really glad my boyfriend encouraged me to start seeing a therapist. I am a very anxious person. I also have some anger issues and have a hard time dealing with and figuring out my emotions. He thought a neutral person to talk to who is trained to help with these situations would benefit me in the long run. My first session two weeks ago was kind of awkward. I don't like talking about myself. The good, bad and the ugly. No one cares. Why do they need to know? But if I wanted to become a happier, healthier, better version of myself, I need to accept the help. The therapist went through what she said were "routine questions" that they ask all patients. She asked if I was abused as a kid. Me...abused...no. I didn't have scars or bruising like I remember sometimes seeing on kids while growing up. Although... Jerk did hit me sometimes and there were the twelve times he forced me to have sex with him. I thought to myself, do I tell her...I remember the first time when he told me if I told anyone no one would believe me. On the other hand, my therapist is a neutral person. She doesn't know my father. I said a quick prayer and I took my chances. I told her everything. It felt so good to get that off my chest. It was painful but at the same time so freeing. I know I will not be able to work through all of it in one or two sessions. I think that in time I will be able to heal and overcome all of this. I need to remember, baby steps...one day at a time...even one minute at a time. I can do this. Prayer time! Thanks Diary!

Love, Me

Today

Dear Diary,

It has been 14 years since my father, aka Jerk, forced me to sleep with him the first time. I have been in therapy for four years now and I wish I started before that. I have learned so much about how my past affects my present and future. Nonetheless just because parts of my past were very negative and ugly, doesn't mean my present and future need to be negative and ugly. I have learned so much about myself, how to deal with emotions, how to love someone else. I have learned that I don't need to shut everyone out and I don't need to let everyone in, either. The most important person in my life is me. I cannot truly love and care about anyone else unless I truly love and care about myself. No one is perfect but I know I am on my journey to be a happier, healthier version of myself. Time to pray!

*"And when we speak we are
afraid
our words will not be heard
nor welcomed,
but when we are silent
we are still afraid.
So it is better to speak
remembering
we were never meant to
survive."*
Audre Lorde

The Long, Winding Path to Peace

Jacqueline

Things were good, at least I thought they were. My five siblings and I lived in a fabulous home in Connecticut with a devoted Mom and a Dad we adored. True, finances had deteriorated with Dad's business but we were managing. My eight years of Catholic school had left me well prepared to succeed at my prestigious high school and as a Sophomore I was taking a tough load of advanced courses and getting top marks across the board. And, I was diving, all the time. As a serious competitive springboard diver preparing for National Championships that spring I was in the pool at least three hours a day. I loved it and my team and my coach were my life.

At home with my five younger brothers and sisters things were hectic and there were some signs of things cracking at the seams, like Mom crying on Sunday nights when Dad left to work out of town for the week, but overall I had no inclination that my life was about to shatter into a million pieces. And then it did.

I don't remember what town we were in, or which hotel we were staying in or even which diving meet we were there for, but I do remember a hotel meeting room with the typical ugly, green and gold color scheme. The room was empty except for chairs stacked along the walls, and it was barely lit.

My coach, Jon, pulled me inside. " I want to talk about my Dad."

Jon had learned the night before that his father had died. I had been there when he got the news. Jon gestured to a chair along the wall, and I sat. He sat beside me. I waited for him to share his feelings, anxious to provide comfort if I could.

I had been at Jon's apartment that night because as usual, a bunch of the team had crashed there to party before heading to a diving meet the next morning. Jon always insisted that we tell our parents that we were leaving for diving meets on Fridays, but went to Jon's place instead of a hotel. In his bachelor pad, a crowded, unkempt apartment over a garage at a local summer pool club, Jon freely offered booze and drugs to six or seven of his elite female springboard divers, all of us between fourteen and seventeen years old. I was fifteen. Jon was thirty. This behavior should have been a warning, but I was genuinely clueless.

Back in the conference room, I sat and waited for Jon to talk or cry or something, instead, he kissed me. I was shocked. Even though I was fifteen, I had never had a boyfriend or even kissed a boy other than playing spin the bottle once in eighth grade. I trusted him, but this seemed crazy. He was my coach and a grown-up. But, there was a part of me that was also flattered that he chose me. After all I idolized him.

I started to relax a bit as he continued kissing me, but when he started touching me in private areas I froze. I was in way over my head. I didn't stop him, but I couldn't bring myself to touch him back.

"Touch me." He murmured. I didn't move.

Jon pressured me harder. "I need you. Make me feel good."

I couldn't speak. I was in a mental panic. Jon was still kissing me and touching my breasts. Occasionally he reached between my legs, but I had squeezed them shut.

"You're not being fair. I'm making you feel good. You need to take care of me. Come on." At that point Jon was sounding frustrated with me.

Finally my panicked mind reached my body, and I yanked my shirt down and ran from the room, saying "I'm sorry" as I left.

I remember very little of the rest of the weekend, but I do remember that I didn't tell anyone. It felt like something that should be kept secret. The week after, I lied in bed at night feeling guilty that I didn't help him "feel good too" as he had asked. After all, I cared about him, and I trusted him. At practice, Jon told us all the time, "I'll never ask you to do something you're not ready for." Of course, this was about trying a new dive, but it seemed like maybe it should apply. I also felt very indebted to him because my family's finances had declined and he was paying my training costs. Finally-- this seems ridiculous now--I decided that I loved him, and therefore, I should do whatever he wanted. This lesson came from my Mom, who always put my Dad's needs before her own. By the end of a few sleepless nights, I decided that if Jon approached me again, I would do whatever he wanted.

I didn't need to wait long. About a week later Jon was driving me home from practice, and he asked me to slide over next to him and put my arm around him. I was so inexperienced I tried to put the arm between us over his shoulder, but of course, I couldn't reach. He laughed and told me to use my other arm and put it around his waist.

We drove to the end of a dark street, and I tried to go along with what I thought he wanted me to do. However, when he pulled my pants off and climbed on top of me in the front seat of his station wagon, I froze again. When he tried to enter me, I screamed in pain. He tried a little longer, but my body wouldn't cooperate, and finally, he gave up and told me how to use my hand to satisfy him. I did, all the time feeling hurt and embarrassed. As soon as he finished, he drove me the rest of the way home.

He never approached me again. I felt confused and ashamed. And alone. Jon never asked me to keep it secret, but I felt I couldn't tell anyone, so I wrote about it in a journal. That was a mistake. If this was all that happened it would have been bad but it wasn't all that happened. Things were about to get much worse.

The following April, two months after the "incident", was YMCA National Diving Championships in Ft. Lauderdale, Florida. My diving team was flying down from Connecticut and staying at a hotel on the Ft. Lauderdale strip across the way from the National Swimming Hall of Fame. I was very nervous about the meet. It's difficult to qualify for Nationals, and I had worked very hard for a long time to get there, training six or seven days a week for at least two years. Due to our financial woes, I couldn't afford to stay with the team. My Dad was doing some business near Ft. Lauderdale and he arranged for me to stay with him. I brought my journal with me and left it at the apartment while I was at the meet.

While I was sleeping at my Dad's place, I was still hanging out and partying with the team. Jon's only rules for us were, "Don't get caught, and don't get on the plane with weed, buy local." I remember climbing over the fence to get into the pool area in the middle of the night to jump off the ten-meter platform. I also remember diving and partying with a girl with no arms. Watching her dive with no arms was amazing, watching her smoke a joint with her toes was hysterical. I competed well and was having a good time.

A few nights into the trip, Dad asked if I would go to dinner with him at the Marina Bay Club, a fancy, floating restaurant on a canal. I was excited to go, as I loved attention from my Dad. We sat down and ordered.

"I read your diary," he said.

"Oh," I said, not sure what he would think but instantly very embarrassed.

"When I first read it I was angry with your coach," Dad said, "but then I spoke to a friend of mine, and she convinced me that you were old enough to know better. That the coach wasn't to blame."

I wanted to climb under the table, and I said nothing. Dad was clearly angry at this point, and I got a little worried. I had never been in any trouble with my Dad and I desperately wanted his approval. He was my hero. As the oldest of six children born in just eight short years, I was my Mom's right hand while Dad traveled every week for business and I believed that Dad appreciated that. He was proud of my intelligence and straight A's. But what would he think of me now. I knew he would be disappointed but maybe it wouldn't be too bad, I hoped, he'll just lecture me a bit and then I can work to win back his trust.

I never suspected anything like what Dad said next. "Now that you think you're old enough to have sex, I can tell you a few other facts of life. The women that I went to advice for about your coach is my mistress. She's not the first either. Remember Ross and Simone?"

Instant panic, confusion, disbelief overwhelmed me but I managed to give a slight nod. Of course, I knew these women. Each of them had worked and traveled with him for many years and I liked and respected both of them. My mind was racing in a dozen different directions. Maybe I was misunderstanding him; I thought with no real hope. This couldn't be true. Why is he telling me this?

Finally, I asked a question. "What about Mom?"

"She knows. We have an understanding," Dad says.

OK, so this was totally unbelievable to me, but I let it pass. "But, why? Why would you do this?"

That question was a big mistake.

As if it was not big deal to be telling his fifteen year old daughter intimate details of her parent's sex life, Dad calmly explained, "I have needs that your Mom doesn't like to meet. I like a lot more sex than she does. She thinks oral sex is dirty. It's her church upbringing and all. She'll do it, but she makes me feel guilty about it. "

Ewww! Then I realized that while he was acting calm he was furious and everything he was saying was designed to hurt me. That was my punishment.

Dad continued justifying his actions. "I still love your mother. I always will, but I have needs. Your Mom is always more interested in you kids anyway. I use to ask her to travel with me, but she wouldn't want to leave you guys. I'd promise to hire the best sitters, but she never agreed to go."

I wanted to say, "So I'm supposed to believe this is Mom's fault?" But I didn't say a word.

I don't remember the rest of the meal. I felt hurt, shocked, scared and so disappointed in my Dad. But mostly, I was devastated for my mother. So this explained the crying, the weekly visits to the therapist, the lack of self-worth. It made sense now.

My poor mother. Things would never be the same again. How would I ever feel normal again? What could I do to help my Mom? Protect my brothers and sisters from this knowledge? Dad's punishment struck deep and irrevocably.

In the days after I got the news that my family was not as it seemed, I was a mess. I couldn't eat, wouldn't speak, even to my friends. I didn't want to be anywhere near Jon either. Luckily, I thought at the time, the swim team coach from our local YMCA, who was also in Ft. Lauderdale with his swimmers, noticed my distress. Charlie guessed what had happened with Jon, so I admitted it. After several days of barely speaking or eating, I told him how my Dad had "educated" me. He was comforting. I felt I had found an anchor and leaned heavily on him for emotional support. A year later, when I was sixteen, and he was thirty-one, he approached me for sex. By that point, I was more experienced, and one could argue that I knew what I was doing, but he was an adult, and I was a child. I should have been able to trust him. Clearly I couldn't.

Continuing the catastrophe when we got home from Florida, my Dad convinced my Mom of his point of view and she looked at me like I was a disgusting and asked me repeatedly if I was pregnant. Neither of them ever saw this for what it was--sexual abuse of a child. Neither comforted me. For years afterward, my Dad would use this to strike at me when he was drunk. His favorite insults were that I was a slut and lower than the scum he could scrape off the bottom of a swimming pool. So, the beginning of the end. The end of innocence, trust, childhood. But still just the beginning, because life would get much worse before it got better.

One tragic result of this string of disasters was that I concluded that people as a whole were guilty until proven innocent. I trusted no one any more. I also hated my Dad and hate is an exhausting all-consuming emotion that does the hater at least as much harm as the hated. For many years I participated in behavior that wasn't good for me, including too much sex and alcohol and relationships with abusive men. But I had a strong survival instinct. Senior year I ran away from home and found a wonderful family to shelter me. I kept up my good grades and graduated Valedictorian. I got a Bachelor's degree and then a Master's in mathematics despite being an emotional wreck much of the time.

Finally I realized that the hate was eating me alive. I need to reconcile with my Dad. It took many years and sooo much therapy but we built a relationship. It was tentative at first and I was very fearful of him at the beginning but I eventually learned how to enjoy Dad's positive traits and protect myself from his negative ones. And as a true Jekyll and Hyde, Dad had some amazing good traits. As with all people Dad was neither all good or all bad. The trick was to benefit from the good and stay sheltered from the bad.

As I matured it became a relationship of mutual respect and real closeness. I was at his bedside when he died a few years back and he asked me to look after everyone for him. I promised that I would. This was both a mark of how much he believed in me, the admiration I had wanted from him as a child finally earned, and an acknowledgment of how much alike we are. He knew that I could fulfill the role he played in our family. Hopefully just the good stuff though!

My Mom stayed with my Dad for his whole life. She says she doesn't regret that. I tried for many years to convince her to leave, telling her that she deserved better, but she always said she would rather have some of him than none of him. I cannot relate to that, but she gets to decide how she lives her life.

Creating successful romantic relationships proved difficult though. I married my first husband because he met the high bar or not being an active alcoholic, not beating me and keeping a job, and, of course, he was a way out of my family. When that failed because, well because while he wasn't a bad guy we had very little in common, I married a pediatrician eighteen years my senior. I thought he would take care of me and he was pretty good at that initially. However, as I grew stronger and more independent, he became controlling and abusive. He demanded sex every day regardless of my lack of interest. It might have been hopeless, but for one good thing he did during our seven years together. He paid for individual and group therapy for me. I began to heal.

When I got strong enough, I left him. No one would abuse me again. Not my father, not other men. No one. From this position of strength, I met my amazing current (and final) husband. He helped restore my faith in humanity. He never pressured me for sex; he let me set the pace. Even now after twenty years together he maintains this posture. Having consistent and explicit control over the decision to have sex has worked very well for me. This dynamic should be a given in any healthy relationship, but we take it a little farther. My husband won't even initiate sex. The most he might say is that he finds me sexy. Otherwise, it's up to me. This may seem unromantic, but it works for us. I didn't ask for this, but he seemed to perceive that I would tense up at times he did pursue me, and he knew my history. It may not be ideal, but given my history it's reasonable.

I feel safe and happy. Our children are safe and happy too. They understand consent, they know my story, and I think that protects them somewhat from becoming victims. I think they will be as caring and respectful as their father. I think they will (or do) make great spouses.

"There is no greater agony than bearing an untold story inside of you."

-Maya Angelou

I Am Woman

Rachel

I am woman
Proud and fierce
Opinionated and strong
Unapologetically intimidating
Intelligent and informed...
Independent
Resilient
I am a lioness
A crown of flowers upon my mane
Earthly and compassionate
But prepared for attack
To stand up for my beliefs
And to protect the people and ideas that matter to
me
I will hold the hands of the women willing to join
me
And patiently wait for the man who will support me
on my quest to become indestructible
My courage brings me power
I will not conform to fit the womanly ideals men
have laid before me
The soft whisper must cease to exist
Hear me roar

Turning the Corner
Angelique

My former boss Sandy called me into her office at the law firm one day after I hurled a filing tray at the wall and scared some of the staff. She got straight to the point.

"If you're not happy with your life, you're the only one who can change it," she said.

No one had ever said that to me. And while I knew what that statement meant, I didn't know how to actually change my life. I was unhappy and felt awful that I could not figure out how to make myself happy. I cried every day for months and could not explain for the life of me why I was crying. It felt shameful because I didn't know how to explain what was happening. All I knew for certain was that I did not like the job I was doing. I did not want to be a secretary any longer. And while I settled for being a follower, deep down I wanted to be a contributor to the world. There was no one I could talk to about my unhappiness because thirty years ago you "sucked it up" or you'd be considered weak.

Even after the filing tray incident, it would take another six years for me to learn how much power I had over my own life. The change was slow, but I took one step in front of the other, not knowing where I would really land. I signed on for weekly visits with a psychotherapist. I started a small business organizing personal documents for customers in preparation for annual tax filings. Also at 33, I began modeling and taking fashion design classes at the Chicago Merchandise Mart. Each activity gave me confidence and made me feel good again. I kept taking steps in the direction I wanted my life to go.

If my former boss (whom I love and keep in touch with to this day) had not made that statement to me some 30+ years ago, those opportunities would not have even crossed my mind. I took steps in the direction of happiness. And when that happened, when I went for what I really wanted in my heart, when I answered the summons, the earth, the Universe, God, Higher Power, conspired to manifest my desires. It took me years to understand the truth of this, but I'm grateful I finally showed up in my own life.

Delusions of Grandeur

Krista

That date I was on that night in October when you walked into my life was already over before you entered the bar. We locked eyes. You and I. An immediate energetic pull of force began. I knew you felt it, too. I saw the twinkle. It first grabbed my heart. And it went straight to my core. It entered my soul. It traveled and trickled and tickled its way down my body. My mind left the universe right then and there. We both had to look away after a few intense seconds.

The next couple of hours we spent flirting, giggling like school kids, and shooting some stick. Usually, I suck at pool. But that third game, I beat you. And you were smitten by that. You're self-proclaimed status as an "excellent pool player" was shattered by some schmuck apprentice. In that moment, I thought we were going to fuck right there on the pool table. But we just kept on with the childlike give and take of random gibberish. We laughed a lot. We kept locking eyes. That pull - that force that beamed from you to inside of my entire being - kept shooting more than the sticks between our hands.

At the end of the night, I found out you were engaged. I should have figured you were taken. You were too beautiful to be single. Too charming. Too nice. Too gloriously and deliciously sexy. You would have cheated on her that night. That much I knew to be true. But I couldn't do that to another woman, having had it done to me before. So we said goodbye and went on our separate ways.

Eight months later, in another bar in a different town, I was dancing to some friend's band. I had been going there for over 30 years. I took a break from the floor and was standing about two feet in front of the door. Anyone that come through, had to pass by me. The door opened many times as several patrons were coming and going. Then the door opened and I glanced towards it. There you were. That guy I never dreamed I would ever see again. The locking of our eyes happened before you even stepped one foot inside. Forcefully, desire overwhelmed me. Again. Stronger than anything I ever felt before in all my life on this Earth. And it traveled through every single inch of me. My legs were shaking and it wasn't from dancing this time.

My knees almost buckled. You could hardly believe your own eyes. Was this some sort of illusion? Stunned at the sight in front of you, we exchanged some words and a hug so powerful that I think it scared both of us. You asked me to join you at the bar. Who was I to decline such a welcomed invitation?

Turns out, you weren't engaged any longer and you were living directly across the street. I wasn't dancing on the floor any longer but my insides were dancing the rest of the night while talking with you.

It was pouring rain that night. I had my friend's pink turbo convertible, a two-seater Mercedes I had borrowed. You asked me for a ride home. I laughed at your request, as you lived just a few hundred feet away from the entrance. But, I gave in to your charming ways after multiple gentle leg rubs. The tingles got me.

We kissed for what seemed like hours and you begged me to come up to your apartment. I wanted to play these cards right. If I went up there, I might be seen as some sort of hussy. And be disregarded like one, too. I declined your advances, albeit as tough as that was for me to do. I was proud of myself. We exchanged phone numbers and you texted how glad you were that I didn't go up there with you. You had said you would have lost respect for me. "YES!" I thought to myself. A little victorious celebration ensued in my brain.

The red flag of knowing you would have cheated on your fiancé that night back in October should have told me to run in the opposite direction. But that pull! That energy! It was in the stars. I was doomed. I fell hook, line, and sinker. Or more like heart, mind, soul, and body.

We texted all day, every day, for two weeks. I waited for you to ask me on a date. That didn't happen, though. I was wracking my brain trying to figure out why you were waiting. You told me things. Many things. You spoke of how you felt when you saw me again the night at the bar across the street. You told me it scared you and you never felt something so strong before. I knew it! You had fallen, too.

I was out late one night and started the trek towards my home when I started to have a reaction to a medication I had started. I felt like I was having mini hallucinations. You were out, too, and in an Uber ride on your way to your apartment. You asked me if I could safely make it there, as it was much closer than me driving to my house. Shit, could I?! My car ride turned into auto-pilot mode and I barely remember the actual drive. I was going to see you again. And that was all that mattered!

You were waiting outside your apartment building for me to get there. We started kissing each other hard as soon we were in close enough proximity with each other. You took my hand and led me up to your pad. All the while kissing our way up the rickety, iron back steps. And once inside, it was on and burned like a wildfire. Hot as hell. But I was in pure Heaven. We went from the kitchen to the couch, our lips barely letting go of each other. I remember staring you in the eyes as I undid your pants for the first time. We couldn't take our eyes off each other, nor our hands or our mouths. You picked me up, cupping me from behind. Me with my legs around your waist ... making out all the way to your bed. You had a lot to drink earlier. And you couldn't get it up. What? *Damn it,* I thought to myself, *this isn't happening!* You said you weren't able to "fully perform". You felt so badly for having an issue down there and kept apologizing for it.

You kept on apologizing to me and then kissing me. And then stopping, and looking at me with that look in your eyes – that beautiful, charming look in your eyes that drew me in the moment I ever laid eyes on them. And then we kissed hard all over again. And throughout the rest of my time there, you kept apologizing to me and looking at me with the same look. I knew it was real. I kept reassuring you that I didn't mind that you couldn't perform. I figured there would be plenty of other times.

I asked you if you were having fun. And you said that you were. I asked you if you were happy in that moment. You said that you were. I asked you, "So then what are you so sorry for?" The moment is all we have. You told me that you were disappointed that you couldn't please me and you looked me dead in the eye. I felt those butterflies in my stomach and those tingles that you gave me down there - the same feelings I got when you walked into the door at the bar eight months earlier. You seemed to walk right inside my body that night.

We fell asleep in each other arms, my head on your bare, beautiful chest. I was sure this was the beginning of something like no other I had ever had or even dreamed of ever having.

But I was so wrong. For the next six months, I was your little text buddy. I would get "good morning" and "good night" texts. I would get so many pictures of you. I would get countless promises of seeing you again. But instead of a relationship, what I really got were lies. I was played. And I hung onto your mere text words. I held onto hope. I figured you were just a tad spooked by the energy we exchanged. I told of you of dreams I had. I told you of signs I saw. I was spooked, too. But not enough that I thought you wouldn't want to see where this could lead. I wanted to experience all the thrills. All the feels. All the fun.

I wondered how long I had to wait. You were all I could think about, awake and asleep. When time passed and then passed some more, and nothing you were promising was actually coming to fruition, I would ask you why you kept me dangling. I would tell you cut that string and let me just go. But you wouldn't do that. I fell into an emotional rut of depression. It sometimes came out in angry texts from me to you. I was hurting. And confused.

I was in love and fell fast and deep. And you knew it.

I couldn't let you do this to me much longer. It was killing me inside. I was letting you walk all over me through the wires of a text stream. You just hid behind your technical device.

And then one day, you just said "goodbye". And you blocked me. I never heard from you again.

It took me months to realize that this experience actually was a gift. You were a player, a liar, and a cheat. What did I really want someone like that for? I didn't. And the Universe made sure I didn't have to endure a real relationship with you.

Do I believe in love at first sight? I guess I do. I've never felt that strong sort of energetic pull and force before. I honestly haven't. Not like that. I am now so glad you really didn't feel it, too. It was all just delusions of grandeur.

My Dad

Ashley

My dad died after losing his battle with heroin.

My parents were inexperienced 17 year olds when I was born, entangled in a whirlwind of premature love. Both of them were still coping with being abandoned by their parents. My mom was left by both of her parents and my dad was abandoned by his dad. My dad's quest to understand how the world worked started like many fatherless African-American boys. His mom worked long hours to provide a home and food for them. She encouraged him to be active in sports and clubs. She tried for years to keep him from becoming yet another number in the system. Somehow, somewhere along the way he gave into the predatory call of the streets that ultimately made him drug statistic.

Throughout my childhood, I visited my father at every correctional facility in Maryland. Long road trips to Eastern Shore, quick trips to Baltimore City, a few visits to Jessup, the next town over, and the dreaded trip to Hagerstown, just to name a few. Despite the circumstance, the visits were always filled with excitement for me as a young girl. I looked forward to spending that time with him and I was excited about the moment we would share. I would anxiously wait to catch a glimpse of him as the officers released him into the large visiting room. The walls and barbed wired fences of those facilities protected those moments I desperately needed as a young girl.

As a teenager I remember calling my dad at his girlfriend's house on one of his brief visits home from jail. Even as a teenager, I was still that girl searching for precious exchanges with my dad. I anxiously waited to hear his voice on the other side of the phone.

"Hey dad," I said, awaiting a response.

"Hey baby."

I noticed a difference in his voice.

That was always his greeting when he spoke to me, and to think about it to this day warms my heart. However, this greeting was almost unrecognizable, it was infested with slurred speech. We tried to continue the conversation anyway. The slurred speech worsened and the conversation was irrational. At one point, he stopped in mid-thought and asked, "who is this?" when I told him my name. He said "who?" I repeated my name and relationship to him. He became angry and said, "I do not have a daughter." Under the influence, he did not remember who I was. I was angry, not with my dad, because even then I realized he was sick. Addiction is an illness. I was pissed off with the gangs and illegal drugs, I knew first-hand how can they prey on the weak and win!

Unfortunately, when my dad eventually died he was trying to reverse the damage inflicted by the vicious hands of the streets. He was in rehab and he was being treated. He was trying to make a change in his life. In one of our final conversations, he apologized to me. He apologized for choosing the streets over his only daughter. He apologized for being weak. I don't know the exact moment, but at some point drug culture preyed on his vulnerability and they took my dad from me before he physically was gone from this Earth.

I despise the streets for what it did to me, for what it stole from me, for what it put me through. The hatred I have for the streets is alive and well, it's the passion that drives my being and my vision. Without ever having to experience that lifestyle, the streets taught me an important life lesson about predators: A predator's easiest casualty is the disenfranchised, one who feels powerless based on circumstance. So, in my life, regardless of my circumstance I never lose my power.

"Painful as it may be, a significant emotional event can be the catalyst for choosing a direction that serves us - and those around us - more effectively.

Look for the learning."

Louisa May Alcott

The Dregs of the Bottle

Lois

Alone in the car, I'm on an especially desolate portion of road when my mind begins to wander. And then it hits me like a gut-punch, as it always does. The memory inspires such a visceral reaction, that I'm overtaken physically. I feel a heat begin to sear, beginning at my collarbones and working its way up my neck – I know my ears are flaming. As the heat rises to the top of my head, a leaden knot begins to build in my gut, creating a nagging, tugging sensation pulling me deeper into the driver's seat.

Coincidentally, I'm on the first leg of a two and a half hour drive to have a maintenance visit with my therapist. Funny enough, the distant memory that jarred me back into the present has nothing to do with the therapy I'm undergoing now; these days, it's all about understanding and healing from the things that took me down the dark path of alcoholism. Look, I own my shit, but there are some things that stick with you forever, you just find a way to calm yourself when those memories and flashbacks pop up, seemingly out of nowhere.

As an alcoholic, having worked my way through each step in a 12-step program, I have no secrets – there's no point, secrets make you sick. I will say, however, that my sponsor is the only person privy to some of my darkest moments, moments that inspire a rapid heartbeat and gut-clenching clarity when they emerge from the recesses of my memory. That tugging sensation in my belly? That hot flash creeping up my neck? Both are the result of the shame I evidently still feel about things I did when I was deep in my alcohol addiction.

I don't feel shame about the stupid things I did, or the risky behavior I exhibited, it's three incidents that took place that are so far out of my character, that I hold onto them, lest I ever think it's a good idea to grab a glass of wine. At least that's what I tell myself, because I'm at peace with so many of the other indiscretions I committed during my drinking years.

After struggling to find myself and carve out a career, I had the uncanny ability to self-sabotage when things were going smoothly in my life. Exhibit

A: landing a sales gig with a fun company that allowed me to make good money and spend my days outside of the suffocating walls of an office cubicle. I made my own hours, I was challenged, and the pressures that came along with that independence fueled what would become a full-blown alcohol addiction.

I was in sales, I traveled frequently, and I was successful; I wasn't responsible. I could cancel appointments when I was hungover and put off cold calls for another day. Worst of all, I worked for a company culture that silently accepted alcoholism and drinking to excess, because, you know, salespeople need to burn off steam.

I was way beyond burning off steam when I headed in for a multi-day sales conference, where I knew I'd be nursing hangover headaches while sitting (suffering) through sessions throughout the day. The evenings were filled with lavish dinners and drinks, lots and lots of drinks. On this occasion, I'd gone far beyond being tipsy, and was blackout drunk when I chatted with a man at the bar, drinking shot after shot, despite already having had enough. It was never enough back then.

The bar closed and we made our way to his room by taking the elevator, me trying not to make eye contact with a colleague who I knew was about to do damage, yet again, to his marriage with the new sales rep hanging on his arm. I followed the stranger from the bar to his room, where we shared even more drinks. I remember him talking about his girlfriend, and not wanting to cheat on her, and I remember being so drunk that I didn't care. We kissed for a bit and then I passed out, too drunk to make it back to my room.

I was awoken by the shrill noise of my phone ringing, after having shut off my alarm clock some time ago. Again and again, my phone rang; again and again it was my boss calling. I was late to the first meeting of the day. By the time I'd dragged myself to my room, my phone was blowing up and I knew that I needed to return my bosses call and clean myself up. Embarrassed by the whole situation, having been informed that the company VP was just minutes from calling the police, I concocted one of the worst, most damning lies of my life – I told my boss that I thought I'd been roofied. And while that, to this day, remains one of the worst hangovers I've ever had, if that guy had roofied me, he didn't take advantage of me.

Even worse, the guy had been living in the hotel for a month, while working on a big IT contract, so he wasn't a stranger to the hotel, and he certainly didn't have a bad reputation. My path crossed his a couple more times during my stay, but I was too ashamed to make eye contact, lest he confront me with the allegations that had been laid out. The fact that I had stooped so low, committing character assassination to cover my own ass, remains with me today.

Alcohol fuels a fire that's slowly burning within the alcoholic, and it's fire that I see when I have flashbacks haunt both my dreams and my waking moments. I literally built a bonfire with my ex-boyfriend's belongings.

If you've ever gone through a breakup, you know it can go one of two ways – smoothly, or mired in anger and hurt. At 31, I thought I'd met my mate, but was blindsided and despondent when he failed to come home or contact me for two days, deciding to break up with me via a phone call (I actually think it was a text, but I blasted his phone until he answered). The worst part was that we shared a house together.

When he did stay at the house after our breakup, it was in the basement, but most nights he wisely stayed away. One Friday evening, having found evidence of his fun, newly single life, I started seeing red. I'd already been drinking, and probably whiskey at that – I'd acquired a taste for it with him – so it seemed like a great idea to start purging his items from the house for him. We'd purchased a fire pit, to bring our love of campfires home, and the sight of this item, an item we'd purchased together, significant because of the many hiking and camping trips we shared, made me even angrier in my spirit-fueled disposition.

Stumbling into the house, I made my way down the hall to the guest room, my shoulder slamming into the doorframe, as I drunkenly miscalculated my trajectory. I threw open the door to the closet, where our suits and formal clothing hung side by side. I was like a bear, my hand a claw, swiping across hangers, pulling tailored shirts, suits and ties out by the fistful, growling with rage as I did so. Armful by armful, trailing ties along the way, I brought everything out to the backyard, and dumped piles of expensive clothing into the fire well, scooping and flipping errant tie ends into the pit. Dousing the clothing pile with lighter fluid, I can only imagine the crazed look in my eyes, as I touched a flame to the chemical/accelerant-sodden suits.

Halfway through my bonfire, it began to rain, the cold drops sobering me up enough to realize what I was in the process of doing (and that there was no turning back). I panicked, spraying more fluid onto the smoldering fabric, in an effort to keep it alight. I managed to burn most everything, clearing charred tie ends from the pit and burying them in the garbage. Months later he would ask me if I knew where his suits and ties went, and I told him that I didn't know. My alcoholic mind justified my answer as the truth, as I didn't know to what landfill our trash was ferried away.

I pride myself in my work, which is why the fact that I was a terrible employee still haunts me. I was living the dream, working for the largest, most renowned publishing house in the world, and I managed to screw that up as well. On paper, my job was ideal, but the reality was that I was caged inside a cubicle, forced to be productive during set hours, and saddled with a boss who managed to get under my skin, despite being located halfway across the country.

In my effort to put my road warrior days behind me, I emphasized the fact that I was ready to settle into a cubicle with this publishing house, throughout my multi-level interview process. Little did I know, they had an outside sales position available, one that didn't require 60 hours on the road a week.

After I was hired, a slow resentment began to burn once I found out that they had an outside position that I was perfect for (but had been passed over because of my very vocal aversion to being on the road all of the time). I felt overqualified for my job, and struggled to accept my lot in my cubicle. As a result, I began to make my own hours, often taking especially long lunches and leaving early to hit the gym before I got my drink on at home.

On one occasion, my boss scheduled a call for 15 minutes before the end of my scheduled work day; knowing that I would get caught on the phone for a half hour or more, that fifteen minute window turning my hour commute into an hour-and-a-half. To avoid getting caught at work, I left early.

Checking my office phone, I found a message from my boss, and called him back, proceeding to drive circles around my neighborhood (I'd told him that I'd hit the road early so I wouldn't get caught in traffic). My boss asked me outright if I'd left work early, but I blatantly lied about how early I'd left work; I'm sure he knew.

Months later, my husband received a job offer in another state, and I happily tendered my resignation, but not without leaving ungracefully. I was mentally checked out by the time I gave my notice. I transitioned my accounts to all of the unhappy reps who had to take over my duties. When they complained about all the additional work, I yelled at them to stop bitching and then I encouraged them to call their supervisor. To this day, I feel a deep shame in the type of employee I was, and the way I handled leaving the company.

Seven years sober, I acknowledge my wrongs, but I don't stay stuck in the past. I know that I did things that were out of character for me, things that were hurtful towards others, and I make amends by conducting my life in a responsible and respectful manner. Am I embarrassed by the things I did when I was drinking? Not necessarily, but I am disappointed in the person I became under the influence of alcohol. I never had any external or meaningful consequences for my actions, which is why I continued to drink as long as I did. Internally, guilt and shame were the ongoing consequences of my actions. Perhaps the most important lesson my alcoholism has taught me is to have empathy for others. As an alcoholic, I know better than to judge my fellow man, because, let's face it, I've done some pretty shitty things myself.

Life with Dad

Hope

Most of what I remember from my childhood was not wanting to come home, dreading what mood my father would be in. I had seen his rage from an early age and it only got more severe the older I got. He would scream and yell, and his veins would pop out all over his head and neck. He would bang his head against the wall and ask if we liked seeing him do that. Then he would tell us that we were making him do that to himself. Or he would pick things up and throw them across the room.

I remember my brother's cymbals crashing to the floor.

I remember the rage. There was a lot of it. And when things were calm we would all tiptoe around to make sure that the storm did not brew up again. We were scared to death of our father. Out of necessity, I took on the role of the peace maker.

I was the one that he wanted to be around most of the time, so I did everything with him. Any passion he wanted to explore, there I was, whether

I wanted to be or not. And I did not feel the freedom or safety to speak my truth to my father, so I pretended that I wanted to jog around the track with him, that I wanted to draw animals, that I wanted to play golf, that I wanted to be in his band, that I wanted him to touch me.

I hated being home alone with him. I hated having to stay while my mom and brothers went to see my grandparents in the adjacent state. I would beg my mom to take me too, but she never did. She just said, "Be good and don't upset him". Of course, my dad would get excited when they left, and I would get scared.

He made up a game. "Let's pretend that I am your boyfriend," he'd say, "kiss me like I am your boyfriend." He continued the fantasy. He would tell me that we could move to Colorado together and start a new life and have children. He would say, "We are going to have so much fun. We can rent dirty movies, and take baths together, and run around naked." The thought horrified me. My father was my first introduction to sex.

When I think about our intimate relationship, I feel a lot of shame. I wish that I could have been a stronger child. I knew from the first moment that the "sexual education" door was opened, that it did not feel right. I wish that I had more fire to tell someone what was going on or at least stand up to my dad and tell him that I knew this was *wrong*. But since my fear of him was greater, I did whatever he said and pretended to be okay with it. I knew one of two things would happen if I spoke up: he would pout and cry, which would make me feel guilty, or he would be angry with me and give me the cold shoulder, which I hated almost as much as him touching me.

The one time that I finally did have the courage to tell him "*No more!*", he locked himself in his room and wailed like a wounded animal for hours. That response scared me even more than his rage.

As I got older, I stopped taking baths, because I knew he would come in and look at me and touch me. I started taking five second showers and hurrying to get my clothes on so that he didn't have any time with me. I was so unhappy, so *disgusted*. The few times that he noticed I was avoiding him, he felt hurt and rejected and started on one of his "nobody loves me, you're just like your mother" routines. Then the cold shoulder, until I said I was sorry and would do whatever he wanted.

The shame of going along with the whole game will probably haunt me forever. Along with the shame that I did not stand up for myself and protect myself.

I knew that I had a few options. And I thought about those daily. I knew that I couldn't go through with killing myself - I had already tried that once and it scared me too much. I knew that I had to eventually tell someone, run away, or kill him. But in the meantime, I did my best to make him happy. In the bathroom, the only place I'd have a few moments alone, I would have pep talks with myself about being stronger. I'd think, *Just get through this a little longer.* Or I would cry my eyes out with rage and stare at myself in the mirror and pretend that I was telling him to his face how much I hated him.

I'm not sure how I was able to make it through the first sixteen years of my life. It definitely made me stronger. I went to some therapy - the state required it. I even ended up in a hospital - my mom took me and left me there.

I don't think that the anger is still there, I'm not really sure. I felt it as it happened, I wrote many poems about it later. More than anything I feel a sadness for not knowing how to care for myself as a child.

My father and I have never spoken to each other about the incidents that occurred in my childhood. The times that we have spoken, we have been more intent on creating something new between us. But it hasn't ever felt completely OK with me because I don't want to move forward pretending all is good, because it isn't.

Having my father molest me has been the most intense experience that has happened in my life. It has played a huge part in molding who I am today. Getting him to talk to me about it would possibly be even more intense.

I wonder if he cares about how I feel. I wonder if he thinks about what it was like for me. I wonder if he will ever ask me questions about how I felt and listen to what I have to say without interrupting to justify his actions. I wonder if he will realize how much he hurt me and be truly sorry. I wonder if he will keep blaming his actions on events that happened in his past. I wonder if he will own up to his mistakes. I wonder if he knows that these incidents are more than mistakes, because they were carefully planned and manipulated and it happened to me on a daily basis.

I also wonder how many other readers are going through this and keeping it a secret. I would like you to know that it is NOT your fault. Please speak your truth. Please listen to that whisper, to that feeling when it says, "this doesn't feel right." Seek out anyone you trust and tell them what is happening. You deserve to be respected, to feel safe, to be loved.

Your voice is important.

Childhood

Maribel

It's not what you did for us,

but what you didn't do that hurts.

Never saying I love you.

(I've always wondered if you do.)

Never saying I'm proud of you.

(I still wonder if you have been.)

I guess you must be.

How can you not?

We were great kids

And we're now great adults

But we've done that on our own.

I don't understand, especially now that I am a

parent.

Knowing that immense love I feel for my son and

wondering how you've been able to withhold it from

us for so long, if in fact you've felt it.

Have you felt it?

Have you loved us?

Have you been proud of us?

Have you ever wanted to hug us?

Spend time with us?

Get to know us?

Experience life with us?

Know what hurts us?

Know what scares us?

Know what we love, like, hate, aspire to?

Ever?!

Why haven't you?

Did it make you feel better about yourself when you made us feel small?

Did it make you feel validated to compare us to you?

Do you tell yourself...

At least we weren't working at 10, right?

At least we weren't starving and we had a roof over our heads... Is that it?

At least we had a loving and caring mother all the time, no?

At least you provided the most basic necessities, something your father didn't do for you. Isn't that so?

At least you didn't beat us, am I right?

We weren't working at 10 to support the family, thank you.

We never starved and we always had a roof over our
heads, thank you.
No, you didn't beat us, but you did ignore us and
neglect us.
We did always have a loving and caring mother, but
I can't thank you for that... We would've had her
either way.
We didn't have YOU!
We didn't then, we don't now, and we never will.
I know that now.
I want you to know I didn't have a happy childhood
Although I did have happy moments
But not because of you
I want you to know that I was terrified of you
I want you to know that I needed you
I want you to know that I wanted you
I want you to know that all my life I have sickly and
obsessively looked for your approval in vain
I want you to know that all my life I have just
wanted to know you were proud of me
I want you to know that all my life I have just
wanted to know you saw me
I want you to know that all my life I have just
wanted to know you cared about me

I want you to know that all my life I have just
wanted to know you loved me
It's not what you did for me,
It's what you didn't do that still hurts.
It's not what you did for me,
It's what you've never done that will always hurt.

I saw fathers in San Francisco today
Fathers changing dirty diapers
Fathers talking to their children
Fathers carrying them on their shoulders
showing them the world
Buying them ice cream and churros
Teaching seemingly insignificant things
While the wee ones paid attention with amusement
Forming bonds
Creating memories
Showing love
I always watch
I always wonder
I always still feel like a child
I always miss what I didn't have
I always want that
And I cry over that milk that never got spilled
Because it wasn't even there

The glass always empty

Then on the bus one day
I saw a father
His face was brown like my own father
He carried a little girl with so much love
Comforted her while she fussed
Held her closer
Gave her a bottle with milk
And rocked her while humming softly in her ear
He whispered that they were almost home
And he smiled into the world
A boy was next to him
Those were his kids and he loved them
Every movement of his body showed it
And I was jealous and felt stupid
And I cried

"In every community, there is work to be done. In every nation, there are wounds to heal. In every heart, there is the power to do it."
Marianne Williamson

The Best and the Worst Day

Rachel

I cannot pretend as though I believe that everything happens for a reason. Most of my life has been filled with trauma and dysfunction so abnormal that it is hard to say the strength that has arisen from it was worth the insufferable pain. At 18, I can remember locking myself in a janitorial closet at work, bringing my knees to my chest as I sat on the trash can, and sobbing to the universe, pleading my case.

A week before, I opened the refrigerator door inside our ancient, rusted trailer to find a carton of blueberries, some wild fish that my youngest brother had caught down the road at his favorite stream, and a small container of mayonnaise. My mother was suffering from a severe bout of depression after my father left for his mistress, leaving her in bed for weeks. She only got up to use the restroom or to ask my brothers and I for another $1.06 so that she could buy herself more McDonald's sweet tea.

So of course, when I realized that I had missed my period that month, I hid myself away to weep. There were so many mouths to feed already and I was only a teenage girl fresh out of high school, trying to make enough money to send myself to school. A baby sounded not only like a death wish, but also like the end to all of the freedom I had ever hoped for. Nine months later (due to what I believed was a high moral compass paired with a strange e-mail from a pro-life foundation), I received the gift I had initially wished away and I named him Conner. The day he came into my life was without a doubt the most incredible day I've ever lived through. The next few years were just like any other new parent's years with a newborn who turned into a sassy, independent toddler full of attitude and energy.

On the day he turned three, I called to talk to him during the time in between my day job and part-time evening job. I knew his father and grandparents would have cake and gifts for him in a few hours while I served spaghetti and meatballs to hurried guests at the restaurant. I sipped on an iced coffee and asked how his day had been. He said very little that made sense, but I wasn't surprised because it's impossible to hold a conversation on the phone with an excited toddler. After I hung up with him, I took a picture of the sunset that evening from one of the screened windows facing the cornfields. That photo is the last captured memory I have before one of my best days warped into one of my worst day.

August 23rd was my incredible baby boy's birthday.

August 23rd was also the day that I was sexually assaulted by a co-worker outside of the place we worked. The day that a man stuck his hand inside of me without consent and pulled out my innocence. That innocence has since been replaced with a fiery feminist fuel, burning to help heal and empower all survivors but first, it was nothing but an emptiness that made my stomach churn even on the best days. Weeks after the attack, I was numb. I couldn't eat, or sleep, or write, or socialize. For the first time in my life, I was forced to ask for help.

The funny thing is, when I started to see a counselor, we didn't spend copious amounts of time talking about how I could deal with the recent pain of what had happened to me. Instead, we worked through my past. We worked through the chaos that was my entire childhood and discovered ways I could cope with the feelings I had never faced. I am still working so hard to become who I am destined to be, without adding on the baggage of my trauma.

I won't pretend like everything happens for a reason, but in the strangest way I feel so blessed to have an August 23rd because without it, I am unsure that I ever would have willingly confronted the person I was before and turned her into such a strong, kindling flame.

The fire will only continue to grow, I will burn brighter daily.

Mommy's Gone

Trina

SUICIDE. It's such a taboo word. I learned that early on. People don't know what to say. So after my mom died I learned to both protect myself and save the other people from potentially uncomfortable moments by downplaying a tragic scenario. I know now that it was my own coping mechanism.

My mother was an amazing woman. But I think everyone saw it but her. You see, my mom suffered from bipolar disorder and schizophrenia. And after multiple attempts, she finally succeeded at ending her life. She was 35. I was 14. My twin sisters were 7.

She told me about her illness when I was 11 or 12. As the eldest... I was cast as mini-mom at an early age. I started to understand that her mood swings were not just her being "fun mom" or "sad mom"... but that she had this burden really a constant struggle... And even more for a single mom with 3 daughters.

And then I did what I later learned do so well. I stepped up. It was the first in a lifetime of "superwoman" moves. I decided it was up to me to help her out. Now that I understood how much she was struggling, I learned to read the signs. I took care of my sisters and watched sadly when the lows came. I learned to ride the "fun" highs – because her manic self was light, carefree and downright silly. She laughed. She sang. She let us jump on beds and stay up late. I would forget that she was sick - almost. She also told me why she didn't like taking her meds. How it made her feel "funny". What a burden for a young girl to bear. But I wore it – for years. It formed me. It made me strong. It turned me into "the responsible one".

Learning about my mom's depression and watching her illness progress was hard to bear. Even tougher was seeing the multiple attempts at taking her own life. The time she swallowed a bunch of pills. The time she cut her wrists and came out of the bathroom with them wrapped in tissue – blood seeping through despite her efforts to stop it. It was horrible. And deep down I think I knew that she wasn't going to be with us for a long time. But nothing prepared me for the moment when I learned that she had jumped off of a bridge. But in an odd twist of fate – she didn't die. She broke her leg in 2 places and was hospitalized for months. She never came home. Ultimately it was a stroke that killed her during that long hospital stay. And that's the 'safe' story I tell people when I can't bear to share the full truth. As a matter of fact, until now, only a handful of people not from my hometown know the full story. I'm not sure why I carried her illness and death as my burden, as my shame – but I did – for many years.

I don't talk about her death much. I talk about the good things. Like how my children both inherited her "upside down" smile – a smirk that turns down at the corners of the mouth. And how I inherited my smarts and penchant for games, puzzles and brainteasers from her. She would make up songs as she would cook. I sang those songs to my children when they were young.

As I matured and settled into my superwoman role, I buried the pain and ignored my shame. As a self-described "overcomer", it was much easier for me to let people assume what they wanted about me - that I grew up in a "normal" middle-class household. After all, I graduated from one of the top schools in the country didn't I? When people find out my mom died when I when 14 I glossed over the details and gave the "safe answer" – and then changed the subject as soon as I could. You know - it's bad enough to lose your mom as a teenager. People feel sorry for you. They applaud you for being brave... for being strong. So I learned to leave well enough alone. To stuff my feelings and keep it moving. To be grateful for the love and support that poured out from my family members – how they swooped in to be there for me and my sisters. And truthfully – they never stopped being there. For that I am truly eternally grateful.

I miss my mom so much! They say time heals all wounds. Maybe. Now the grief takes a different form. It blindsides me. I may be having a good day – and then something triggers a memory. Like a song she used to sing. A scent. Or my kids give me a look that makes me think of her. Mostly it's good memories that make me smile. Sometimes it's like getting hit by a Mack truck. WHAM! And I am flat on my back, or sobbing. Like now. Special milestones are hard too – like big birthdays or graduations.

The truth is... I do believe that God is somewhere in the midst – among the pain, among the mess and the angst. And He sends people to fill the void – like my many, loving, fantastic family members. I occasionally get reassured by people who knew my mom growing up. They tell me how much I look like her, and how proud she would be of the three of us. I know that she is smiling down watching us flourish – knowing that others stood in the gap for her. That gives me comfort.

If you are like me, and you lost someone to suicide or other tragedy, I encourage you to let it go. Please put down your burdens – it's not yours to carry. There is nothing to be ashamed of. Life can be tough, and we all do the best we can. But you deserve to be happy, healthy, and free. If you are struggling yourself – I implore you to do what is necessary to take care of yourself.

Talk to someone.

Get the help you need.

Please.

National Suicide Prevention Lifeline

Call 1-800-273-8255

Available 24 hours everyday

You Hurt Me

Charlie

you hurt me

and it was not okay

i was too young

for the things you did to me

you were supposed to protect me

to take care of me

but instead you touched me...

THERE

over and over again

and you knew it was wrong

and i carried the hurt and shame for years

i never told a soul

how YOU HURT ME

i bet you don't even remember...

but you know what?

I'm done feeling ashamed because of what you did to me.

It's YOUR problem, NOT MINE.

"I write about the power of trying, because I want to be okay with failing. I write about generosity because I battle selfishness. I write about joy because I know sorrow. I write about faith because I almost lost mine, and I know what it is to be broken and in need of redemption. I write about gratitude because I am thankful - for all of it."

Kristin Armstrong

Little Girl

Dena

little girl
wipe away your tears
forget your past
and leave your fears.
it was not fair
the life you lived
but it's over now
so try not to care.
the hands that fed you
hurt you too.
so many times you wished to die
in the bloody tears you cried.
you never had to play this role
sheltered from the outside world
and confined in another's soul.
you cried for help
so many times
no one understood your pleas
wrapped up in their own crimes.
stupid games.
don't let him win.
break the mental chains
that constrict you to the horrid world you dwell
in.

run to us,
we will protect you.
you must learn to trust
those who will not
hurt and desert you.
everyday i was with you
though you never knew-
each stab
pierced me through.
i felt the walls
come crashing down
on the life that never made a sound. but bravely
you grew.
cruelty of a man
more than you could handle
so you burned him with
what you knew
and held for 8 years long.
but now you've spoken
And you are not wrong.
smiling at the blood
dripping down his face-

pulling him under giving him a taste.

now the nightmare is no more the storm is
gone.
you may still be sore
but it won't last long.

play
And hold tightly to
all he wanted to throw away.
search for others
who
suffer in the world
you once knew.

**"*Write what disturbs you,
what you fear,
what you have not been
willing to speak about.
Be willing to be split
open.*"**

Natalie Goldberg

Coming out of the Basement

Hannah

I am not fond of basements. I used to think that basements were for protection during storms or to play in when you're a kid. Unfortunately, I learned pretty early on that our basement was my dad's place to molest me, to hide, to keep secrets, to hold a gun to my head and say those words "I will have to kill you if you tell." Some words never leave a five- year old.

During my early childhood I also thought chocolate was made for ice cream, not for a penis. I now hate to see a Hershey can swirl on white ice cream. It still creates a picture in my mind I'd like to forget. Perhaps that's why I always choose butter pecan or cherry ice cream now. It's so sad that some of the most innocent things from my youth were taken away from me by my own father.

He negatively impacted my life in many ways. My molestation hit me hard in my late teens after I decided not to keep a baby I felt I was not fit to raise. Abortion is still a word I barely say to this day. I ran from being a mom and the additional shame it would bring since I was not married.

I grew up excelling in anything that took me from that home. I became a pro at having a boyfriend to fill some very empty gaps in my heart. The longing to be loved always led to feeling worse, especially after sexual encounters.

For the longest time, even as an adult, I would move on before the familiar feeling of hurt would start again. I eventually had two failed marriages and many abusive relationships. I just kept running. I ran just like that teen version of myself who eventually said, "No more" to her father. I never stopped running until I found a secure place.

Gratefully, one day things in my life started to change. I got a new job after years of therapy and self-love. I met a special man after about six years of "me" time. The words that finally split open my heart were, "When are you going to let someone love you?" I gave in, allowed true love into my life, and finally ascended out of that dark basement of pain.

These days I refuse to run, even if problems arise. I know that no one is perfect, but I confidently refuse any form of abuse or unkindness in my life. I stand my ground and only accept sincere love.

I am at peace because I have forgiven the past and I have forgiven my father. I made this decision to heal in order to live a full life. I am no longer satisfied to just survive.

Through the years I have been blessed with three daughters, one son and seven grandchildren- so far! After so much heartache earlier in my life, I am also happy to report that I have been married to my best friend for 16 years in 2017.

I am finally finding harmony and connection in a way that I didn't know was possible for me! At times I still struggle to trust others, but I have come a long way.

Since I have a very loving husband, I can finally relax and enjoy our life together as we age. Instead of running away from my past, I now embrace all of the beautiful opportunities I have to make new memories. Ironically, my husband and I even love "run away" together on one adventure after another!

I have found faith love, forgiveness, and my family. I have come out of the basement of my past and I pray that everyone who reads this understands that they, too, have the power to make a new life for themselves.

You deserve love and happiness.

"If you are a woman, reading my tale, learn to fight for your rights and the respect you deserve as a human being. But, if you are a man, reading my tale, learn to respect women and, likewise, advocate for them."

Yanan Melo

When You Run my 5K

Herisme

A few years ago in our town, over a very short time period, there were three ladies who were brutally murdered by their husbands. Two of these husbands also murdered their own children. The third intended to, as far as I'm concerned, but wasn't given the opportunity, so he just killed his family's cats, his wife and himself instead.

So now our community runs 5K's in their honor to raise awareness and money for victims of domestic violence. Well, we run them for two of the white ladies, and one family's children. The third woman and her children were a lower income Hispanic family, so our subtle, not so subtle, racist community doesn't run for them. But, that's another topic for another day.

What kind of husbands, fathers, sons, uncles, men do this? Men who are sick. Men who are crying out for help in ways that go unheard. Men that are abusive, controlling, ill, and violent in such duplicitous ways that their neighbors and communities, even their own families and spouses, consistently describe them as the "nice guy next door."

How do I know about these things? Well, I suppose when you read our story in the local paper or the little paragraph on our sign-up genius/donations webpage, you'll get filled in. Maybe you won't know about any of it until you show up to support our sponsored cause at our memorial 5K, which might be your first 5K and you'll feel all the community support by signing up for the cause. "Oh my, how sad. I think that I saw them at a thing once when they did something."

I know these things because I've seen it happen before.

I know these things because my husband is very sick.

I know these things because my husband wants to murder our son and me.

I know this because he said so.

Not, "I'm going to kill you for not putting out the trash, you knucklehead." More like, "I am your apocalypse, I'll make you drink my blood, I'm Sly Stallone, Our 3 hearts beat as one, and I know God doesn't forgive murder." You know, he wants to LITERALLY, in the truest sense, kill murder kill us.

Let me tell you, um, yikes. It is extremely scary, and life altering, no matter how sick you know a person is, to know that this other human being wants to hurt your child and you merely for being who you are, for existing.

"Get a lawyer," you say?

"Call the police," you say?

"Get him to a hospital," you say?

Done, done and done.

Here's the catch though, none of these well-intentioned institutions can actually protect us.

"No, no!" you say?

"You must not have followed the correct procedures.

You must not have said the right things.

You must not have filled out the correct police reports.

You must not have found the right Doctors/hospitals/lawyers, because if you had, you and your son would be safe."

Indulge me with a moment of your time to dispel these lovely, comforting, and overly confident in naiveté myths for you – decimate your glorious happy bubble.

The lawyer may file papers for you, provide legal advice to you regarding the laws in your particular state, navigate your local court. Your lawyer has to work with all of the other lawyers, judges and court personnel long after your legal issues are over, and therefore will not be vigilante advocating for what you think is "right" all Hollywood style. Also, your lawyer has heard and seen every disgusting side of humanity, most likely, and can only represent actual proven truth – not conjecture, predictions, heresy or those dreaded feelings of yours (tip: see your therapist for those fun times). What you vehemently insist is non-negotiable and the most important things for you and your child, may not match up with the actual laws of the land, and may not be within your lawyer's capabilities. Not because they are incompetent, but you will know this because of your lawyer's undeniable extreme competence and professionalism – both of which you will need if you need a lawyer at any time in your life. Also, lawyers are not superheroes with any superpowers, other than super negotiating finesse and super law knowledge.

There's a funny thing about the police too. They cannot arrest or detain anyone because you suspect something or are frightened of something. They need actual proof (gasp!) to do either of these. If someone uses their words, like, I don't know, "I'm going to murder you" and such, yet they don't actually murder you, the police cannot arrest that person. As told to me, "words are just words, not actions," and "if every written threat to kill someone equaled an arrest, most people on Facebook would be in jail."

Hospitals, Mental Health professionals – hey, guess what? They are even funnier than the police and tighter bound than the lawyers. HIPPA – google it, as it is AWESOME in a so very not awesome way for anyone with an adult loved one who has a serious mental illness. Also, as an adult, no matter what your condition regarding mental illness, your self-reporting is absolutely the only information that the Mental Health professionals can and will take into consideration. Psychotic much? Okay. Do you feel homicidal or suicidal? Not right now, you say? Okay. Do you want treatment? No, you say? Super! You are clear minded, discharged and free to go. This also frees the hospitals and Mental Health professionals from adhering to any bugaboo "duty to warn" an intended target (insert me, our son) for a psychotic homicidal mentally ill patient (insert my husband), because they just verbally confirmed that the patient can verbally say they are not homicidal right then.

"No, no, no, no, no," you say. "That cannot be. I know that the hospital can commit someone and detain them."

Sure they can, until the adult patient says they want to go and don't want to hurt anybody or themselves. The adult patient who two days prior sent multiple homicidal threatening emails prompting a Protective Order through the court system, after being picked up by police for threatening to blow-up the hotel he was staying in and to physically harm housekeeping, yes, him, indeed. Clear minded and well = discharged.

"Wait a minute," you say. "Is this the same guy who was picked up by the same police for erratic and disoriented behavior within 36 hours of being discharged from the hospital after a nine day forced stay?"

Thusly I say unto you, "yup."

And so, what are we doing right now? How are we keeping safe?

We have a protective order. It's like a restraining order, except it begins with the letter, "p."

We have had open communications between local domestic violence groups, child protective services, police, sheriff, pediatrician, therapist, school, workplace, lawyers, family members, close friends, church etc. so that everyone is aware of the situation.

Words, words, words, words, words.

Here is the thing about words.

They cannot actually physically protect you.

Here is the truth.

When someone wants to murder you, nothing can protect you.

Repeat

Nothing can protect you

Nothing can protect.

Nothing can.

Nothing.

You can pray. You can hope. You can peek around every corner waiting for the something awful to happen. You can file every paper, you can contact every agency, you can spread your story far and wide, but absolutely nothing can protect you.

You cannot run away because a psychotic adult can hire an almost unethical lawyer to prevent that, especially since you have a child together. You know, because the law protects parental rights. Even for a murderer. Or, in this case, a wannabe murderer.

More awesome-sauce for this hearty party...

Have I mentioned that our son is being forced to attend supervised visitation with his father, who incidentally, in case you misunderstood something previously read, wants to murder us and we have a protective order from a judge in a court showing they believe his father is too dangerous to be around him?

No? Well, it is true.

So not only has our son been frightened of his father's behavior because of our previous domestic violence in the home, and his father's attempt to hurt him because I refused to allow him to hurt me anymore, but also now re-traumatized each week by being forced to sit in a room with him for an hour and listen to his father's manic nonsense.

"Son, your father is too dangerous for us to be around him, except you're still going to have to sit with him for an hour in a room each week and be subjected to his psychosis."

Our son is six years-old.

Anyone else finding this uncomfortable, barbaric and unbelievable?!!?

Any else feeling like this might be truthiness/movie pitch/rantings instead of reality?!!?

Me too, except I AM ACTUALLY LIVING IT.

For now.

Until we are murdered by my husband

and then the police can actually arrest him,

and the Mental Health professionals will be forced to treat him,

and the lawyers can move on to their next case

and y'all can carry on planning and running our 5K.

When you run my 5K, you should expect tastefully decorated and chilled bottles (not plastic, duh) of water, with matching, tastefully decorated gluten-free, dairy-free cupcakes, which will, of course, have some kind of added unexpected nutritional value ("oh my! I would have never known kale was in there if you hadn't told me! Amazing!). And napkins. Cloth commemorative napkins, which could maybe double as a glow kerchief or brow sweat mop, as you desire.

As you round the corner to the obscene amount of brilliant festive balloons (clear with floating glitter inside, white ribbon) and giant silky white ribbon indicating the finish line, someone, most likely my irreverent Uncle or sardonic brother, will point you in another direction, yelling, "Just kidding, this is a 10K all the way! Run it for Mrs. X and Little X! Go, go, go, go, go!" And you'll do it for the cause *fist bump*!

Psssst.... Just a thought. If my husband could have actually received appropriate quality mental health support and guidance, my son and I probably wouldn't be murdered.

I guess then, though, you'd miss out on my sweet tale and my lawyer would be about $50K short.

Tra-la

Love, Mrs. X and Son X

Addendum: My husband was arrested in our backyard due to three violations of the current protective order. He resisted arrest, and now has four criminal charges to face. He was uncooperative at the jail and at both bond hearings, so he has now been transferred to a state hospital for mental illness treatment to determine if he can be held accountable for his crimes. These are misdemeanor charges and he has no prior criminal history. The good news is, he will probably be held until his trial date on November 19th at 8:30am. The bad news is that if he is competent, he goes to court that day, he will probably be released. So, we're right back to "still not murdered" status until...? Try Thanksgiving weekend for our 5K – everyone will want to run all of that turkey off, so you'll get an awesome charitable turn-out. xo

Like Playing With Fire

Estelle

"Let me play with your fun bags," Tom* said often, most times with no one around. But, occasionally, he harassed me in front of other coworkers who could "take the joke" and not file a complaint to HR on my behalf.

Even when I would push back on Tom's advances, he turned quite belligerent, or ignored me altogether, and I truly hated both--especially the latter. So, in an effort to keep the peace, I allowed Tom to do and say as he wished. Frequently.

My first day as a bank customer service representative (CSR) was in early June 2007. I was informed that each of the other CSRs would take his or her turn training me over the next few weeks. During that time, I learned when, and how, to properly answer the phones. *Pick up before the second ring*, I was reminded. *Make sure to announce your name and ask how you may be of assistance.* I learned how to quickly and efficiently open new accounts, cross-sell products, and complete other necessary tasks.

Although I completely disagreed with Tom's work ethic, which was to do the least amount of work possible without getting fired, I was intrigued by him. I longed for the few times he trained me, and later, I aimed to be as close to him as possible.

I found Tom only mildly attractive, but he could charm his way into a padlocked box. Tom had a knack for making even serious situations funny. Plus he made me feel attractive and, frankly, wanted. My boyfriend struggled with complimenting me, so I welcomed Tom's attention.

Over the first year that I worked with Tom, his words and actions shifted. "You look great today" turned to "I want to see you press your tetons on the vault door," which then turned to "Be my gumad." High fives turned to him "accidentally" grazing my arm and neck, which turned to air-humping me from behind. I played along with most of it, even the most extreme remarks and behaviors, but never acted on anything.

He'd say, "Be my personal fluffer" and I'd ask, "How would you like it?"

We engaged in this type of pattern several times a shift. One time, though, about a year and half in, I tried to end the perpetuation of his weird obsession.

"Come to the vault. I want to see your knockers," he directed.

"Not right now. I have a lot to get done."

"Just do it, you prude."

"I have to help the customer who's waiting." My eyes begged him to not make a scene.

"Whatever."

He answered like it hadn't bothered him. But, I knew him well enough to know he was actually pissed, and I hated that. He didn't look me in the eye or speak to me for over a week. And during that week, my attempts at "reconciling" just resulted in him slamming doors, walking away from me, or making nasty comments under his breath.

For the next fifteen months, I played in his game of emotional chess: I carefully picked my moves, navigating the fragile space between physically cheating (a place I wouldn't go) on my blissfully-unaware boyfriend, and being belittled or ignored in front of coworkers and customers. It was a game that I really didn't want to play but was too tired to fight against.

In January 2010, I finally transferred to a new branch in my new town, an hour away. I figured I could leave my past in the past. Tom had other plans.

For the next year, Tom continued to e-mail and call me through the company's internal networking. He continually invited me over to his house--when his wife wasn't home--to "catch up." I always agreed, knowing that he might pursue something more. Sure enough, his wife would return while I was there; I forced myself to explain my presence there, while he remained motionless and silent. He pegged me as the scapegoat for his marital problems. Eventually he started pressing for pictures. I refused every time. Until the time I didn't.

I sent him two shots of my right breast, popped out of my tank top, no face included.

"Bazoinga!!!" he texted.

Shit, what I am doing?! I thought. Still, Tom and I continued playing our game for a while longer.

The winter of 2011 quickly came around and I was invited to Tom's new house. I made a wrong turn down a very secluded, wooded area. Because of the packed snow around me, I was forced to drive forward. Then I got stuck. I called Tom to rescue me, and after an hour of him digging me out of the snow, he and I finally had to face his furious wife.

Less than two weeks later, right before my 25th birthday, I received a phone call from a number I didn't recognize. I let the call go to voicemail. It was Tom's cousin who asked me to call Tom, as soon as possible, on the landline number provided in the message. When I called, Tom answered and informed me that he and his wife had been going through "some stuff." He told me that he lied to her about the kind of pictures I sent him months prior, that it was an "art project" for which I needed his opinion.

He told me that we couldn't have contact anymore, that he'd reach out in the future, after she moved past the crazy notion that he cheated on her. Tom and I never once had a sexual encounter, yet that phone conversation made me feel like the dirty gumad/mistress he wanted me to be all along.

This past December marked five years ago since that phone call, the very last interaction with Tom. Confessing to my boyfriend (now husband) never happened, and so I still live with the regret and shame--shame for being manipulated, shame for playing along. So much shame for being emotionally unfaithful to my partner and causing even more distress in another person's romantic relationship. To admit that the relationship with Tom was the most toxic--and twisted--I've ever been in is to admit I am flawed.

Amidst my flaws, I have learned from my experience, learned to be careful with whom I interact. I know it's okay to not trust so easily, yet trust in my relationship with my husband and the foundation we built years ago. I recognize now that my refusal to play along with harassment is not weakness, but instead strength to confront what is wrong. Perhaps one day I may also have the courage to release myself from any remaining shame that still resides within me.

The Family Secret

Vanessa

Charlie,

You truly have been the love of my life for 16 years! We share an amazing life together with our two beautiful children. I have let you see me, the WHOLE me.

Except this one piece...

I need you to listen, just listen.

Please try to have an open mind and take my feelings into consideration. This is extremely difficult for me to tell you, as I have NEVER told anyone this before. I am your wife, and this has been such a heavy weight to carry. For so long, I have hidden this secret with me. And I can hide it no more.

You ask why my family hates my father so much, and I have been lying to you about the reason why. I am so sorry. I tell you again and again that they just don't get along. I have never told you the TRUE reason. I still keep my father's secret, for fear of people not seeing him for who he is.

MY FATHER. The man who raised me since infancy, who had been the center of my whole world before you, that this man also has a dark and evil side. For most of my life he has been abusing his family physically and emotionally; my mother, my brothers and sometimes me...

My father also molested my cousin Lily when we she was just a child.

Back then, I didn't *truly* understand. I still don't. I don't understand how a *grown* man can do such an *evil* and *disgusting* thing to a child. A sweet, beautiful, innocent child. My father was not the first, nor was he the last "man" to violate my cousin's innocence. Maybe this is why she thought it was okay to molest me.

Because of what my father did, my family was torn in two. On one side my father, the man I loved! The other side, everyone else. Things were never the same once he hurt Lily. With my mother battling her chronic addictions, and my dad being sent to prison, there was just my brother Sam and I left to hold our family together.

I was so young, I didn't understand what was happening. My father was my world. He stepped into this father-figure role when I was just weeks old. I wasn't told until I was 16 years old that he wasn't my biological father. He was, and still is, all I have ever known.

I knew right away that I couldn't tell anyone about what he had done. This became the most embarrassing family secret I've ever kept. I felt alone, dirty, and unloved. So much so, that at times it felt like I couldn't breathe anymore. I wanted it all to end.

Once I took an entire bottle of prescription drugs. Another time, I tried to cut my wrists right in front of my mother, but she barely acknowledged me or what I was doing.

I was only 12 years-old.

I can see now that my mother was just as broken as I was. At the time, I didn't know how she had been through similar abuse herself. All I knew was that I had nowhere to turn; no one to reach out to.

So there it is.

The secret, that holds more secrets...

Please don't hate my dad. I couldn't bear the thought of him not being a part of our lives. He loves you, our children and he loves me.

The man he was then, is not the man you know today. I need you to know the whole truth so we can heal as a family.

"Your problem is how you are going to spend this one odd and precious life you have been issued. Whether you're going to spend it trying to look good and creating the illusion that you have power over people and circumstances, or whether you are going to taste it, enjoy it and find out the truth about who you are."

Anne Lamott

Dear Diary

Scarlet

October 9th

Today was amazing and it was just like I pictured it would be. It was my fairytale wedding, only more beautiful than I could have imagined. I know it took me 13 years to marry him, but you have to understand it's hard living with someone who has a bi-polar disorder and refuses medication. It has definitely been a roller coaster all these years, but I really feel like we are in a good place now. It took years of counseling and varying doses of medicine to better our relationship. Once he finally agreed to consistently stay on his medicine for a year, I agreed to set a date. It's such a relief to know he is on medicine and treating his illness. He is such a great man when he can think clearly. Geez, I love him. He is a great dad to our daughter and such a loving husband. I finally feel like everything is right in place; right where it should be. Today is the day I dreamed of since I was a little girl.

Love,

Love Struck

February 15th

Well, it's been 5 months since I said "I do" and I feel like something is off a little. I'm wondering if his medicine needs to be adjusted. I know if I bring it up, it might start a fight. Parts of me thinks it's just my imagination, but then I see signs of his bi-polar kicking in again as it was before he was medicated. He is spending a lot of our money on ridiculous things we don't need. It's hard being married and having a joint bank account now. I feel like as soon as I deposit money, it's gone on car parts or computer games online. He is always on that computer and so late at night sometimes. I hate having to go to bed alone and not together. I have my personal savings account that I try to stash money in when I can. He doesn't know about this account, but it makes me feel more secure. I'm such a saver and he is such a spender. I guess this goes along with the territory of married life.

Love,

Frustrated

September 2nd

It's almost been a year of marriage! It's always a work in progress, but I do love him and can't wait to celebrate our first wedding anniversary. He really does care about me and our sex life is great. I love having a man I am comfortable with and I love to dress up in lingerie for him. He always makes me feel so pretty even when I think I have flaws. To be honest, I love finding ways to keep the spark going, especially since we've been together as long as we have. Sometimes during the day, I'll send him pictures of me that I would die if anyone saw. They make *me* blush, but I know they make my husband happy. He completes me and I finally feel like everything in my life is just the way it's supposed to be. I have this sense of peace within myself and a sense of accomplishment in my life.

Love,

Still going strong

September 6th

Today was awesome! I got to see Oprah Winfrey! My friend got 2 tickets to Living the Life You Love weekend and she and I went. It was so inspiring to see Oprah in person and listen to her talk. Oh, and it's official: I have a new woman crush, Elizabeth Gilbert! OMG, her story is amazing and she is so brave to have endured what she did. Her message to everyone was to listen to the whisper in your ear even if it's faint. I love her and her message was great, even if it does not seem to apply to my life but I still think she is a phenomenal woman!

Love,

Star Struck

September 15th

So today started like a regular day, I was getting ready for work, while my daughter was preparing for school. We were rushing around like every other morning! I kissed my husband goodbye as he left, pulled out some hamburger from the freezer for dinner... and as I'm getting on my shoes, it hit!

THE WHISPER!

I tried to ignore it. I tried to laugh it off. I started to think I was crazy, but that little voice kept getting stronger and stronger.

It was telling me to get on my husband's computer.

I listened, and went up to our bedroom and opened his laptop. As it turned on I admitted to myself that I didn't have any idea what I was looking for. I started clicking through things while second guessing why I was even on the computer.

Then I saw it!

In his search history was a pornography site. I'm not that wife who cares if her husband watches porn, and sometimes we watched them together. But something about this site seemed off. This site was different; on the screen was not a stranger, it was me! Videos, pictures, private intimate pictures that were supposed to be for his eyes only flashed before me! I suddenly noticed the number of viewers: 12,000. The whole world had access to these photos! I felt my stomach clench. I felt myself start to get sick, I wanted to scream, I wanted to cry, but in that moment my whole body went numb.

I didn't exhibit any emotions as I suddenly heard my daughter screaming to hurry so she wouldn't be late for school. I quickly signed off the computer promising myself to deal with this later and get my daughter to school and get myself to work. I dropped her off and then drove myself to work hoping I would wake up from this nightmare. Tears flowed down my face. Is this really happening? My husband, whom I trust, love... who is *so* jealous and protective of me when any other man even looks my way.... Is it possible that he put every video and picture I have ever sent him, and every one we ever made together, on a public pornography website?

Love,

Betrayed

September 16th

Yesterday was a hard day for me. I could not stay focused at all. I wanted to call him on the phone and confront him, but then I also wanted to search through his computer some more and see what else I could find. I couldn't keep this all bottled up, so I called our marriage counselor and set up an emergency appointment. We talked, I cried, and I told her how betrayed I felt. We reviewed the warning signs to this recent behavior. I explained how I thought he had been off, but I wasn't sure. She explained that sometimes part of bipolar disorder is sexual outbursts or abnormal behavior. She also explained that this does not make his behavior acceptable. Furthermore, because it was apparent that he was off his medicine, I should to act with caution around him. If he was un-medicated, he could be dangerous and I needed to make sure I only approached him in a public place. I explained to her that I wanted to find out all the dirty secrets he had been keeping from me. I wanted to know the websites I was on *before* I confronted him. She told me that I was stronger than I thought I was and that I could do this. We decided we would talk every day until I was ready to approach him. Until then, she said to pretend to be an actress. Act like everything was normal so that I could build my case and get the protection I needed.

Love,

New Actress in Town

September 25th

It's been two weeks since that appointment and it's been the worst 14 days of my life. I feel like I married a stranger! Being intimate with my husband was so hard yesterday. In my head, I kept telling myself "I'm an actress." I found pictures online that he had taken while I was sleeping in the nude because our room is so hot. I was disgusted to see that he had conversations with other men online who were commenting about how hot I was and asking him to send more pictures. He had pictures of himself that made me want to vomit at the thought of someone else seeing him.

I truly feel like I am married to a stranger and all my trust is gone. It's now time to make a huge choice. My mind is made up. This is something I will never be able to forgive. I know myself and I know that I will never be able to trust him again. I'm filing for divorce. I need to tell him.

Love,

I need a lawyer

September 26th

Today was long day. I talked to a lawyer today. I started the process and I cleared my secret savings account out to pay for the divorce. The lawyer is filing for absolute divorce so the process will be quicker since this situation qualifies. I was scared of how my husband would react to the news and if he would even leave the house if I asked him to. The lawyer and I went down to the courthouse and the judge granted me an emergency protection order for him that will force him to leave the house under the grounds of stalking me in my sleep since he was taking pictures of me and posting them on the internet.

After the lawyer, I went home and waited for my daughter to get home from school and took her to get ice-cream. Before I left, I flipped all our wedding pictures and family pictures on the walls backwards. I feel betrayed, how could he do this to me, to our daughter, to our family? I don't know if I will ever know why he did this to us, but I *do* know this break-up will break my daughter's heart.

I'm not ready to tell her. I know, I'll just tell her that daddy has to go help take care of his grandparents at their house because they are sick.

The police officer called me when they came to the house, they served my husband the papers and gave him 15 minutes to pack his bags and move out. After they were gone, I went back to our house; the house I bought on my own. This is the house we built our family in but is now full of heartbreak and betrayal.

My husband called me despite the orders tonight and wanted to talk to me. I told him I just wanted to know why he did it. He said he really has no idea and he was so sorry, he said it made him feel good to hear other people tell him how good looking I was and it made him feel happy inside knowing I was a trophy wife for him and that others wanted me. He said he realized how wrong it was and he can't believe he did it. He admitted that he stopped taking his medicine about 6 months ago because he did not like the side-effects. He said he was going to get back on his medicine and seek medical counseling. At this point his apologies feel too small and don't change my feelings of mistrust. I let him say goodnight to our daughter and then I hung up. I'm broken. This pain is unbearable.

Love,

Betrayed

October 9th

Today would have been my 1-year wedding anniversary. Instead of spending it together celebrating, I spent it in court filing for the final protection order. This was not the way I thought this day would go. Wow, one year, how your life can change so much. This time last year, I was saying "I do" to a man I loved, trusted and wanted to spend the rest of my life with and today I am left with pieces of my heart to pick up.

How will I ever tell my daughter?

I'm not... not yet, that is. How will I be able to provide for myself and my daughter on one salary? I've worked too hard to struggle. Will this pain I feel ever go away? How can you hate someone so much, but hurt and love them at the same time? I spent our wedding anniversary agreeing to go to the movies with my daughter. We wanted our daughter to still think everything was fine and daddy was just staying at his sick grandparents' house at night. Playing house is hard. When I look into his eyes, I see him so full of remorse for what he has done. When he looks into my eyes I'm sure he sees the pain he has caused and the wounds that will never heal. I hope he has started to accept that we will soon be divorced. We ended the night with a hug goodbye and I could feel the tears flow down my cheeks. Wow, what a difference one year makes!

Love,

Heart Broken

May 31st

It's been awhile, but I've been getting used to being a single mom, living on my own, healing from the pain, going to counseling, working and pretending my daughter's daddy is still at his grandparents. He still comes over a few times a week to see our daughter and we are trying to be the best co-parents. He has been going to counseling every week. In addition to bi-polar, he was also diagnosed with sexual OCD and is now back on medicine. I did end up telling our daughter that daddy and mommy are not getting along, so he is going to stay at his grandparents for a while. She burst into tears begging me to reassure her we wouldn't be getting a divorce. Being in elementary school is so hard for her to understand such big adult matters. She said at school they have a divorced parents' group and she does not want to miss her lunch like some of the other kids do and go to a divorce group. My heart broke and I lied. I told her, no we are not getting divorced. She asked why am I not wearing my wedding ring anymore and I told her I just forgot to put it back on from the shower. I lied to my daughter at that moment to protect her feelings, and then decided to start wearing my ring again.

Earlier today was a very emotional day. We had our final court day and the judge signed the order and declared the divorce final. Both my ex-husband and I were crying. That was it, it was over in matter of minutes. I looked down at the diamond ring that no longer symbolized a marriage, but now symbolized security for my daughter that I will continue to wear even though the divorce is final. I feel like the ring is a form of protection over my daughter's feelings; I want her to stay happy and whole. It's also a layer of protection around me because only a handful of people know we got divorced; I need some privacy right now. And finally, this ring is protection from others trying to date me since I'm definitely not ready for that. My ring feels like protection because I am not ready to tell the world the betrayal I went through. I'm still so confused. Is it bad I miss him? Why did this have to happen? I see him now on medicine and in treatment and I wonder if I did the right thing with the divorce. But at the end, I feel safe. I feel protected. The house, my daughter, my bank account and now my feelings and emotions. I know I did what I had to do in that moment and I feel good. To the world looking in, nobody will even know we got a divorce and I don't have to face the world with my decisions I made.

Love,

Feeling Protected

February 15th

It's been 10 months and every day I am feeling stronger and stronger. My ex-husband is still doing well. He still receives counseling every week and he's still on his medicine. Our daughter still does not know we are divorced and neither does the world. We do family events together and see each other all the time. At times, it's like nothing even happened, but through my counseling I have learned to let go of the pain and I forgive him. Sometimes you forgive people for you to be able to move past it and heal and that's what I chose to do.

It's crazy how medicine makes such a big difference in someone's actions and behaviors. I have grown to be stronger than I ever thought I was in the last year. When being strong is the only option, that's what you become...strong!

He asked if he could take me out on a date for Valentine's Day, I said yes! I know this sounds crazy but I still love him and I don't think someone else should get him at his best now that he is in treatment. I went with him for Valentine's Day and it was perfect. Is it weird that I am feeling like I am dating a whole new person? He has changed so much, but for the better. We had our first intimate moment since before the separation, it was magical with no flashbacks. I think I'm starting to fall for him again. Am I crazy?

Love,

Maybe I am crazy

August 18th

For those who say time heals, they are right. I have been dating my ex-husband now for 7 months and he is now moving back in after over a year of being divorced. Life seems to be returning to the fairy tale life I imagined when I got married years ago, only now we will live happy as a divorced couple. I know to the world this sounds crazy, but that's why the world does not need to know we are divorced! Not our families, not the majority of our friends, not even our own daughter, just my ex and I. I've learned a lot in the last few years. I've learned to always listen to the whispers, no matter how soft the whisper sounds. I have learned to be strong when being strong is my only option. I have learned that when I feel like I won't make it through the pain, I will. I also learned the power in forgiveness, even if you are only forgiving them so you will be able to heal. I learned the importance of feeling protected and at ease and confident with my decisions even if I think the world would not agree with me. I learned how to love when I thought I would never be able to feel that again. I am still learning each and every day and I know that this secret I carry may shock so many, but the lessons I have learned from it and strength I gained is worth the pain. I don't ever know if I will get married again. I'm content in my life and I have a sense of peace.

Love,

New Life, New Me, New Us

"I think the associations people have with kindness are often things like meekness and sweetness and maybe sickly sweetness; whereas I do think of kindness as a force, as a power."

Sharon Salzberg

Snippets

Christine

That's all I can remember.
What is wrong with me?
Addiction.
Mental illness.
Suicide.
Abuse.
Ghosting.
Lies.
Something is not right here.
Trauma.
I am fucked up.
Bulimia.
Suicidal thoughts.
Chronic illness.
Codependence.
Debt.
What is wrong with me?
Surrender.
Waking up.
Healing.
Beauty.

There is nothing wrong with you.
There was something wrong with them.

Let it be.

Turning Point

Jennifer Louise

My turning point moment came a few years ago. One day as I lay in bed, I was unable to get myself together. I knew I had things to do, but I just couldn't get up. This had been going on for weeks. I had entered one of the worst depressions I have ever suffered. While I was in bed, I began to have visions of my body on the bathroom floor covered in blood. I saw myself writing the words "I'm sorry"....I was writing it in my own blood. As horrifying as this is, I'm sure you are wondering what I was sorry for.

The list is quite long: I was sorry that I was not the woman my husband expected me to be. I was sorry that I was scatter-brained. I was sorry that I was fat. I was sorry that I didn't make enough money. I was sorry that I didn't have a traditional job with fancy benefits. I was sorry that I couldn't keep the house clean enough. I was sorry that my cooking wasn't as good as his mother's. I was sorry that I was selfish for wanting to have a social life. I was sorry that no matter how hard I tried, I couldn't do things the way he wanted. I was sorry that I wasn't sexy enough and he didn't want to be intimate or affectionate with me.

By now you may have guessed that I was not suffering from clinical depression, I was depressed because I was in an abusive marriage. This bathroom premonition was a gift. The idea of being bloody (and dying?) disturbed me so much because I had never contemplated suicide before. But there was something so alluring in the vision that I knew this was a very dangerous road to be on. Something deep in my soul started to stir, it was whispering to me that *no* man was worth losing my life over.

I spent the next several years working on myself. I realized that I needed to learn my own self-worth and to love myself. I had to discover why I allowed people in my life to treat me as "less than." I also wanted to understand why I, a fairly educated, outgoing, beautiful woman, seemed to attract abusive men. Through my work, I had to go through all of the significant events in my life.

The memories could not have been clearer: one night the cutest guy I knew was at my house. Boy, did I have a crush on him! We were in my living room and I remember he turned on the TV.

He then asked me to come sit next to him. As we sat next to one another, he kissed me and then began to take my pants off and touch me. I had butterflies, this cute guy was making me feel sooo good. Too good, actually. His attention made me feel like a bad girl.

That's really all I remember of that night. The emotion is important here; I felt like I did something wrong. I had a very strong feeling that I was *bad*. As a 45-year old woman I now know I didn't do anything wrong. You see the cute guy was my 16-year old babysitter and I was 6 years old when he took advantage of me.

What I have discovered on my journey of self-love is that I repeated this submissive role with men over and over in my life. I had always allowed men to do what they wanted to me, as if I didn't have a say. I never felt that I could stand up for myself. I had lost my voice.

I am here to tell you that, as women, we can rise up from anything! I have spent years strengthening and learning about myself. I now teach woman how to do the same and to overcome their past while helping them to discover what their true purpose in life is. We then find their perfect balance of passion and experience so they can start a business that gives them the freedom from their past.

Grandma

Crystal

"How lucky I am to have something that makes saying goodbye so hard."-Winnie the Pooh

It has been said that where there was great grief, there was great love, and that it was. My grandmother was a character; a hardheaded woman with a soft soul, a heart of gold, and a humor to make a sailor blush. She fought against many things in her life, and won, yet no battle was bigger than the victory that took her life.

I loved my grandmother, and she loved me. I have always been the type to take care of those around me, regardless of age, gender, or relationship to me. Though I tend to come off as quiet, maybe dark and twisty, or even serious, everything seemed effortless when it came to being with my sweet old lady, or as she was lovingly referred to, my old goat. When I felt like the world was turning against me, or that no one cared about me, Nan was there. When I needed a break from reality, Nan was there, and when there was no one else who wanted me around, I knew my safe place was with her. Over the years, a few health obstacles arose for her including two separate strokes which severely limited the proper functioning of her hands, OCPD, her continuing struggle with her past addiction, Hepatitis C, and finally the beast of them all: small-cell lung cancer. I remember when she was diagnosed: she had been having some chest pains and when the results came back, she told me she had a choice and that was to either be sad or to laugh, and that is where I gather my inspiration from. She was diagnosed in late March of 2015, and spent three months slowly and painfully slipping from me. It became a struggle to try and force her to eat and keep herself alive. I remember feeling so ashamed because I was struggling with so many things on my own, and I did not always willingly make time for her. I became irritable and rude at times because it was the only way I could express how truly terrified I was. On the day she passed, I remember watching her and while my heart was breaking for everything I was losing, I just wanted her to go already. There was a moment of lucidity where she looked at her sister, my aunt Linda, and just begged for God to call her home. I felt so ashamed and so mad at myself that there was nothing I could do; there was always something I could do. In this past year and a half, so much has happened in my life that makes me proud, yet breaks my heart all over again, because I do not have my rock to run to. The most valuable lesson I walk away from her passing with is that you never know the value of even a single breath until you are struggling to breathe.

When someone you love is diagnosed with a cancer that you watch kill them every day, being a caregiver begins to take a toll. When you are left to continue taking charge for everyone else's well-being while still caring for this person and your own cup is barren, stress begins to show. When you are a single mother struggling with the declining condition of one of the only people who ever truly loved you, you start to wonder why you couldn't do more. Was it because you genuinely could not, or did you not try hard enough? I question myself every day. Did I try hard enough, was she comfortable enough, was I good enough, did she ever internalize my frustrations, born from fear and stress, and label herself as a burden because of me? There is nothing I wouldn't do to be able to take that frustration back.

"**Love truly does have the power to transcend evil. It can get us through the most unspeakable of events and give us the strength to keep on putting one foot in front of the other.**"

Naomi Benaron

The Straw that Broke My Back

Greta

I grew up where alcohol was a weekend routine for my parents. Both parents would drink. Dad got tired and mean. Mom got wired and bitchy. To be clear, my dad physically hurt my mom but never hurt his daughters...physically.

I say physically because the ramifications of the drinking, the abused mother, the fighting and the broken promises left scars on my sister and me to this day. I could tell you about an 8 year old girl, awoken from her sleep, who had to serve drinks to her mother and listen to her all night long while dad slept. I could tell you about how mom had to wear a turtleneck to a family Thanksgiving in 85 degree weather to hide the strangle marks. I could tell you about dad hitting mom and her screaming. And my Uncle, who was living with us, taking my sister and me out of the house for ice cream so we would not be there. But the story I am going to tell was the last straw!

My sister often spent weekend nights over at a friend's house. It was a great way to protect herself. With parents that worked, from an early age I handled many things around the house and grew up quickly. At this time, I was 17 years old and close to graduating high school. We lived as an upper-middle class family in a nice area. I had my own car, participated in school functions, did volunteer work and had a part-time job. My grades were good as I was a solid, dependable student. I never got in trouble. I followed the rules of home, school and society. No one knew what I dealt with when I was at home. To be clear, it was not horrible all of the time. Mostly, we lived the dream life. We ate dinner as a family. We talked about our days. We were rewarded for good grades and helping. We went on family vacations. We were encouraged to follow our dreams. We never spoke of the unspeakable things that have and would continue to happen in the house.

This night I lay sleeping in my bed. A figure stood above me seeing if I would wake.

When I did not acknowledge her she shook me awake and said, "I need you to come out here, quick."

I rose from my bed as I had done many times before and followed my mom to the kitchen. In an explosive manner my dad came busting through an outside door. He had been outside defacing my mom's car. As he pushed through the door, he had his gun in hand. He was ranting and raving using profanity directed towards my mother. My mom stood behind me holding me in front of her. You got it, I was a human shield. I just stood there taking all of this dysfunction in. I had spent my childhood hiding this secret home life from everyone just as the rest of my family did. I rarely had friends stay the night at my house. Well, you understand why. I did spend some nights away at friends but not like my sister did. She always had something to do away from the house and who would blame her. So I am standing in the kitchen as a human shield when my father realizes that I am here. He immediately tucks the gun in the back of his pants.

He looks at my mom and says," You woke her up, didn't you?"

My mom responded, "No, she heard you and came out here."

My dad grumbled a few words and walked by us to go to sleep. That is what he did. He would drink, have enough and then want to sleep. My mom would drink and then "nag" at him which caused him to get mad and then violent. That was the end of the encounter with my dad for the evening.

Then came the next phase of planning. My mom and I would plan how they would separate and live apart. A dream that never happened. Of course, this was all while she drank. There was a time when my sister and I were younger and began serving her water because we poured out all of the alcohol. That was not received well. But this time she drank and we talked. We discussed dad getting help and mom agreed. Finally, I was able to go to sleep.

I woke in the morning to parents that were sorry for their actions. Many times I would get something, could be money or a gift, just because they said I was a good kid. This time was different. Mom and I discussed dad getting help and I wanted to help and support this process. This was the day that was going to make the difference. I approached my parents about how we will proceed as a family.

What organization should we contact for help? Was it AA? Now I mentioned appearance earlier. We never let anyone know the private things that happened in our family. Well that is what I was smacked with.

My mom said, "Your father can't go to a place like that because he owns his own business. What would people think of him?"

Now this is not the first time mom and I discussed plans to help that never happened. But this was the straw that broke the camel's back. I began to yell at them saying this will never change. I went out front and sat in my car. My boyfriend, who is now my husband, drove up as I was crying in my car. I got into his car and sobbed. He is the only person I ever told what happened besides my sister. He just held me and let me cry. As we were sitting in the front yard, my mom came out and told me how inappropriate it was to be crying in the front yard. What would people think? She instructed me to go inside. This is where I really began to find my voice because I said no. I drove away with my boyfriend. That was the day that changed my life. I did not find all of my voice at that time but enough courage to make a change.

I have 3 things I would like you to walk away with:

·   When you meet someone, whether they are a child, teen, or adult, remember that you truly do not know what they have gone through unless you have walked in their shoes.

·   If you are in a situation that is less than desirable, do not let that define you.

·   Lastly, do not let your true strength only come out in a crisis. Embrace the power within you all the time.

"I'm here. I love you. I don't care if you need to stay up crying all night long, I will stay with you. If you need the medication again, go ahead and take it—I will love you through that, as well. If you don't need the medication, I will love you, too. There's nothing you can ever do to lose my love. I will protect you until you die, and after your death I will still protect you. I am stronger than Depression and I am braver than Loneliness and nothing will ever exhaust me."
Elizabeth Gilbert

Afterword

Elizabeth Gilbert described a voice that she heard when she was at her lowest point. Surprisingly, in the moment she felt most alone, she heard a message of comfort and connection.

When she heard that voice, she knew that deep within her was a soul that had always been with her and would always love her. Regardless of her pain, her soul had remembered her greatness.

This book project has helped me see how we each have loving souls that whisper inspiring ideas of strength and perseverance even as we experience pain. That internal voice is what reminds us we are loved even when our world contradicts that security.

If there is one theme that runs through this book, it's that we have beauty within. Declaring our wisdom, power, and compassion are ways that we can claim our beauty and align with our soul's desire.

Only then can we hold a mirror up for others so that they, too, can see how much good is inside us all. We must listen to the whisper, believe that we are powerful, and then help others do the same.

Thank you to all of the women who worked on this project, believed in the power of healing, and shared their stories.

We are all living the human experience the best way we know how. It is my hope that we are learning how to love ourselves more completely along the way.

House of Ruth Maryland

All profits from the sale of *Stuff I've Never Told Anyone* will go to House of Ruth Maryland. It is one of the nation's leading intimate partner violence centers, helping thousands of battered women and their children find the safety and security that so many of us take for granted.

Intimate partner violence can happen to anyone regardless of race, age, sexual orientation, religion, ability or gender, and can take many forms, including physical abuse, sexual abuse, emotional, economic, and psychological abuse.

It impacts individuals, families, workplaces, and communities. Since intimate partner violence is framed within the global issue of violence against women, it is shaped and supported by societal, familial, and cultural norms and is complicated by the intersection of other cultural oppressions.

House of Ruth Maryland was founded in May of 1977 by a coalition of women's organizations, religious groups, service providers, and elected officials to provide a safe haven for victims of domestic violence and their children. In November of 1977 they opened Baltimore's first crisis shelter for these victims in a row house on North Calvert Street. The shelter was staffed by one paid staffed person and a voluntary Board of Directors.

In November 1998 a new 84-bed shelter and 6 apartment transitional housing, featuring expanded services and programs, opened. The new shelter has a holistic health and wellness program, including an on-site health clinic staffed by the Johns Hopkins University School of Nursing.

Today, House of Ruth Maryland is recognized as one of the nation's most comprehensive domestic violence centers and has a staff of more than ninety. Their voluntary leadership consists of a thirty member Board of Directors and an Advisory Committee.

Find out more at http://www.hruth.org

Contributing Authors

Leann Rhodes

Rachel Hinkle

Christine Zalokar

Lauren B. Stevens

Angelique McFarland

Ashleigh Mills

Regina Powers

Jennifer Engelmeyer

Crystal Pettis

Sherry McCoy Quinones

Maribel Rubio

Trina Ramsey

Christine M. Estel

Jacqueline Parks

Krista Guardi

Regina Powers

Lesley Morton-Ramsey

Jennifer Land

Acknowledgments

Thank you to all of the wonderful women who showed up to participate in this writing project! We wanted to own our voices and our stories and that's exactly what we did. Our goal was to shine light on our shameful memories so that we could see that those pieces of our past didn't have as much power as we once thought. Ultimately, we wanted to remind ourselves of our strength and worthiness.

This book was also developed through the efforts of volunteer editors. A huge thank you goes to Erika Lane, my right-hand woman. Thank you also for the editorial efforts of Lesley Morton-Ramsey, Suzanna Brehm, and Jessica Jokisch.

-Amy R Brooks

Amy R Brooks loves working with first-time writers who have a message to share. She knows that given time and permission, most people can grow and heal through sharing their wisdom.

Find out how you can work with Amy at
VoicePenPurpose.com

Learn more about illustrator and designer, Abe Kane, at **AbeKane.com** or AbeKaneDesign@gmail.com